RENEWAL

THE PUBLIC SQUARE BOOK SERIES
PRINCETON UNIVERSITY PRESS
Ruth O'Brien, Series Editor

RENEWAL

FROM CRISIS TO TRANSFORMATION IN OUR LIVES, WORK, AND POLITICS

ANNE-MARIE SLAUGHTER

PRINCETON UNIVERSITY PRESS

PRINCETON & OXFORD

Published by Princeton University Press
41 William Street, Princeton, New Jersey 08540
6 Oxford Street, Woodstock, Oxfordshire OX20 1TR

press.princeton.edu

Library of Congress Cataloging-in-Publication Data

Names: Slaughter, Anne-Marie, 1958– author.
Title: Renewal : from crisis to transformation in our lives, work, and
    politics / Anne-Marie Slaughter.
Description: Princeton : Princeton University Press, 2021. | Series:
    The public square | Includes bibliographical references and index.
Identifiers: LCCN 2021012190 (print) | LCCN 2021012191 (ebook) |
    ISBN 9780691210568 (hardback) | ISBN 9780691213460 (ebook)
Subjects: LCSH: Social change—United States. | Social values—United States. |
    Change (Psychology) | Resilience (Personality trait) | Organizational change. |
    BISAC: BUSINESS & ECONOMICS / Leadership | POLITICAL
    SCIENCE / Women in Politics
Classification: LCC HN59.2 .S5823 2021 (print) | LCC HN59.2 (ebook) |
    DDC 303.40973—dc23
LC record available at https://lccn.loc.gov/2021012190
LC ebook record available at https://lccn.loc.gov/2021012191

British Library Cataloging-in-Publication Data is available

Editorial: Eric Crahan, Thalia Leaf
Production Editorial: Terri O'Prey
Text Design: Karl Spurzem
Jacket/Cover Design: Will Brown
Production: Danielle Amatucci
Publicity: Maria Whelan, Kate Farquhar-Thomson
Copyeditor: Madeleine Adams

Jacket art by Dan Cristian

This book has been composed in Arno Pro with DIN Condensed display

Printed on acid-free paper. ∞

Printed in the United States of America

10 9 8 7 6 5 4 3 2 1

*For my sons, my nieces and nephews,
and all the young people in my life.*

*May you live in a world renewed,
and may you help renew it.*

Let America Be America Again

Let America be America again.
Let it be the dream it used to be.
Let it be the pioneer on the plain
Seeking a home where he himself is free.

(America never was America to me.)

Let America be the dream the dreamers dreamed—
Let it be that great strong land of love
Where never kings connive nor tyrants scheme
That any man be crushed by one above.

(It never was America to me.)

O, let my land be a land where Liberty
Is crowned with no false patriotic wreath,
But opportunity is real, and life is free,
Equality is in the air we breathe.

(There's never been equality for me,
Nor freedom in this "homeland of the free.")

. . .

O, let America be America again—
The land that never has been yet—
And yet must be—the land where *every* man is free.
The land that's mine—the poor man's, Indian's, Negro's, ME—
Who made America,

Whose sweat and blood, whose faith and pain,
Whose hand at the foundry, whose plow in the rain,
Must bring back our mighty dream again.

Sure, call me any ugly name you choose—
The steel of freedom does not stain.
From those who live like leeches on the people's lives,
We must take back our land again,
America!

O, yes,
I say it plain,
America never was America to me,
And yet I swear this oath—
America will be!

Out of the rack and ruin of our gangster death,
The rape and rot of graft, and stealth, and lies,
We, the people, must redeem
The land, the mines, the plants, the rivers.
The mountains and the endless plain—
All, all the stretch of these great green states—
And make America again!

LANGSTON HUGHES (1936)

CONTENTS

PREFACE: LET AMERICA BE THE DREAM THE DREAMERS DREAMED

For the past five years, Americans have lived in a state of continual crisis. Our adrenaline is depleted; our adjectives for outrage and incredulity are dull and stale from overuse. Partisan politics has dramatized a bleak landscape of division, without nuance, reckoning, or reflection.

Beneath the surface of parties and politicians lie deeper and unalterable forces of demography and technology, roiling not only the United States but the world. Many countries are confronting systemic racism, mass unemployment, and growing economic inequality, exacerbated by the gravest global pandemic in more than a century and an accelerating threat to the livability of the planet.

Many countries are also facing deep challenges to national identity. For Americans, 2026—only five years from now—will be the 250th anniversary of the signing of the Declaration of Independence. In 1976, Americans in power—the Bicentennial Commission and other worthies—had no ambivalence in describing the year as the 200th anniversary of the founding of the nation. In 2026 that confident certainty will be hard to find. Many Americans will likely think of their ancestors who were not included in that founding. Indigenous Americans may look back to the ancient tracks of their ancestors many millennia ago; Americans who are descended from enslaved Africans may think back to the disembarking of a ship in Jamestown in 1619; Latinx Americans, Asian Americans, and Americans of many other ethnicities may look for their own stories in the grand national narrative.

2026 will be a year of celebration and commemoration, but also of questioning, listening, arguing, and reflecting. Who is US? Can "we"—all of us—embrace a far broader set of traditions and cultures as American, even as we still make room for those rites and rituals deeply embedded in European-American history? Will it be possible, once we come to understand that no one group can be accurately described without a hyphen, to give them all up and just be American?

This book seeks to answer those questions. It is part personal essay, part reflection, and part manifesto. Although it speaks to the tumult in the nation and the world, it begins with events much closer to home: my own experience of crisis and change. As I describe throughout the book, an external upheaval in my life led to an internal reckoning and, ultimately, to a journey of renewal.

I am well aware that mine is a privileged tale. Many people whom I know or read about have had far worse crises in their lives: injury, illness, oppression, violence, exile, and aching, unimaginable loss. Still, I hope that you will find in my story traces and echoes of your own, and thus that you will imagine what renewal could mean for you.

My larger goal is to encourage us all to reflect more on what individual experience can teach us about the path to collective renewal. We often forget that personal transformation can illuminate and inspire social change. The analogy is apt, for to transform themselves, organizations, communities, and entire societies need to do many of the same things that individuals must do. They must face both the past and present with radical, even brutal honesty. Yet they must also preserve what is worth preserving. They must take risks and build resilience. Their leaders, at every level, must develop new ways of leading and sharing power. And they must be able to look forward to a genuinely new future, a dream that everyone can share.

I hope that my experience and knowledge—as a scholar, leader, entrepreneur, public commentator, feminist, and foreign policy expert who spent thirty years focused more on the world than on my own country—can guide you in thinking about renewal on multiple levels and in moving from one to the other. As the author of a book called *The Idea That Is America* and as CEO of an organization called New America, I have been thinking hard about American renewal for many years. More recently, the staff at New America, as in so many institutions, have steadily demanded that all of us live the principles we profess to the world in our relations with one another, requiring a process of organizational renewal as well.

Before proceeding, given that the book moves across many levels and addresses questions of personal and national identity, let me add a word about my use of the pronoun "we." In 2012, when I was fifty-four and had just left a two-year job in the State Department that I had always wanted, I wrote an article in *The Atlantic* titled "Why Women Still Can't Have It All" that went viral.[1] I suddenly found myself on the speaking circuit, talking to audiences mostly of women across the country about how far U.S. society still needed to travel to achieve gender equality.

In many question-and-answer sessions, I quickly realized that the feminist narrative that I had grown up with—the Betty Friedan–inspired story of suburban women home with their kids who had to fight to join the working world on a par with men—was a story limited to white women, and relatively affluent white women at that.[2] Black women have almost always worked, often as the primary breadwinners of their families. Immigrant women from many different countries and cultures have had no choice but to work alongside their husbands to give their children (and themselves) a better life.

I learned, far later than I should have, to be much more conscious and careful about using "we" to talk about all women, or, indeed, about all members of any group. That universalizing "we" is more often a mark of power and privilege than of solidarity. "We" have that privilege precisely because someone is choosing to invite us to speak or to publish our writing. Therefore, as a leader, writer, and speaker, I now try to explain what "we" I am talking about as quickly as possible and to speak for others as little as possible.

In moving from the personal to the political, the book assumes an unorthodox form. I piece together memories, reflections, and research in a structure that owes more to fiction than nonfiction, to novelists who tell their stories from many different perspectives at once. Think of it as a serial narrative, inviting you to add pieces of your own.

When I imagine you, my reader, I imagine first another woman, perhaps an affluent, white, straight woman like me, but I hope also many women who are very different from me. I think particularly of the thousands of women I have spoken to and the millions I have written for over many years, women of my own generation but also the extraordinary generation of young women who are coming into their own in so many ways—inspired by women leaders from the boardroom to the operating theater, director's chair, classroom, campaign trail, and now the vice presidency.

I am writing equally for men, however—men like my father, brothers, friends, colleagues, sons, nephews, students, and mentees, as well as men everywhere who embrace change. Many of you may feel that the masculine ideal you grew up with needs revision and renewal. Parts of this book seek to complicate and challenge the traditional stories of pioneers, cowboys, and explorers who shaped the United States, but not to erase them.

Politically, I lean left. But for those of you who lean right, I remember you in so many auditoriums as I crisscrossed the country seven years ago, arguing for the value of care and the importance of our families. We often found a patch of common ground there. I hope we can find another in shared loved of country.

Demographically, I trend old and white. But for younger readers, white and of color alike, you have the greatest stake in a world renewed. Moreover, all of you will face moments of humiliation and despair at some point in your lives, when you will need to learn how to run toward the criticism and seek renewal.

Nationally, I am American, with old Virginia and North Carolina roots on one side and first-generation Belgian family on the other. At the national level, this book focuses primarily on American renewal, but for those of you outside the United States, I hope that you find insights that you can apply to your lives, your organizations, and your nations.

For Americans, we do not need to agree, and almost certainly will not on many points. What matters is that we can face and accept a common past—told and held by *all* Americans, even as we bear its weight very differently—and imagine a common future as a plurality nation.

RENEWAL

INTRODUCTION

When Leadership Means Having to Say You're Sorry

It was the worst day of my professional life.

I rode the train from Princeton to Washington that morning, lead in my stomach, reviewing and editing my remarks one last time. Waiting for the elevator in my building, I squared my shoulders and arranged my face to be able to greet our receptionist and other staff members on the way to my office. At 2:00, I made my way down the stairs and into our main event space to speak to a packed crowd of well over one hundred employees, with dozens more listening in by phone.

I took a deep breath and began with an apology. New America, the organization I led, was in the midst of a full-blown crisis caused by an employee's accusation that we had decided to fire him and his colleagues due to pressure from a funder. The accusation was neither accurate nor fair, either with regard to New America or to the funder, but it was calculated, successfully, to create a media storm and to put New America and my leadership in the worst possible light. "The result," I told the staff, "has been a set of events that has damaged New America's reputation for intellectual integrity and independence in the public eye, a reputation that is our lifeblood. I stand here now not to defend but to apologize to all of you that this episode has imperiled the extraordinary work we do and to figure out what I and we can do to repair the damage going forward. I'm sorry."

For the next ninety minutes, I answered tough questions from the floor and from current and former New America fellows on the phone, including celebrated writers and investigative reporters. One young employee asked, given several bad communications decisions I had made, how could the staff trust my future decisions? Another wondered why I had waited so long to take action against the employee in question. All I could do was to acknowledge that although I had not done what I was accused of, I had mishandled the entire situation, and to reaffirm that I was ready to listen and learn and do the best I could to grow and improve.

Toward the end, a seasoned Washington hand stood up to say: "This doesn't happen in DC; leaders don't apologize and answer hard questions." Perhaps half the room broke into applause, but the rest sat on their hands. A few members of my leadership team also stood up to speak and share responsibility; others remained silent.

The days wore on. When I look back, the time is a blur: my senior team, our hard-pressed communications staff, our board members, all of our staff who had to explain and defend in response to questions from their families and friends—we all just kept putting one foot ahead of the other. We responded to the crisis as best we could while also doing our daily work.

The essence of the attack was the claim that I and New America were intellectually corrupt, bowing to funders' demands at the expense of our objectivity. The media gleefully repeated the charge without examining how much of our work was and is deeply critical of concentrations of power in our country and our willingness, since our founding, to speak truth to power, regardless of who funds us.

In the trial by press, thirty-eight out of thirty-eight media accounts found against us, accepting that we had actually given in to explicit or implicit funder pressure. Many of those critics were people I knew, people whom I thought would not assume the worst of me, at least not without talking to me first. My Twitter feed soon disabused me of that idea. The things being hurled at me—and through me at New America—were so ugly and so impossible to respond to in 140 or even 280 characters that I quickly realized sanity lay in staying off social media altogether.

I forced myself to go to various events in DC, with my head held as high as I could manage. I wrote as many of New America's friends and supporters as I could, to explain what had actually happened. In turn, I treasured daily messages from friends, and often just acquaintances, who took the time to tell me about a similar experience they had gone through and to offer support and encouragement. Others were silent. Did they not know? If so, I was glad, and certainly did not want to spread the word. Or were they waiting to see which way the wind would blow, a favorite Washington pastime? Worse, did they actually think I was guilty?

Between September and November 2017, I knew that my job was on the line, and rightly so. I was responsible for an organization of some 150 people—thinkers, writers, researchers, community activists, and technologists who worked alongside finance, operations, human resources, development, and communications teams. In the worst-case scenario, if the foundations that provided most of our funding were to stop that funding, livelihoods, careers, and families could be on the line. The work we do, important work of policy research, advocacy, and experimentation on subjects such as education, care, political reform, work-life balance, open and secure technology, and foreign policy, could be imperiled. The New America board had to decide whether the best response for the institution as a whole was to fire me and start fresh. Some board members had been in on the initial decision to let the employee go, but regardless, we were in a mess and I was the leader who had gotten us into it and failed to respond in ways that might have mitigated the damage.

Amid what felt like an earthquake to those of us at New America, the world continued. Hundreds of thousands of Rohingya refugees were pouring over the Myanmar border into Bangladesh. Tensions between North Korea and the United States continued to mount. Facebook announced that it had found five hundred fake Russian "troll" accounts that it was shutting down. A gunman killed fifty-eight people and wounded many more in a mass shooting in Las Vegas. We all reminded one another that what felt so momentous in our world was a very small blip in the larger universe.

Personally, I was in a very dark place. October is always a period of the year when the shortening of the days presses on me like a physical weight, when I must summon all my energy to ward off what other family members and I refer to, jokingly but not so jokingly, as "the rising tide of despair." The technical term is "seasonal affective disorder," or SAD; the reality is a creeping sadness that tracks the waning of the light. I usually fight it with exercise, extra sleep, and time with friends, but now I was trying to keep my chin up for others at New America while staring down a black hole that seemed all too real. My husband, Andy, my siblings, my parents, and even my sons were there for me as they always are, but to little avail.

I knew, objectively, that my troubles were small in the larger scheme of things, that I had far more to be grateful for than to worry about. Still, I was a fifty-eight-year-old woman who had left the security of a tenured professorship to run a nonprofit organization, who had left a foreign policy career to focus more than half of my time on domestic issues, who was the lead breadwinner in my family, who had always prided myself on my integrity and independence—and who was now adrift. In the early morning hours when the gremlins of catastrophic thinking take over, I could see it all come tumbling down. I would be disgraced and out of a job on grounds that would make it very difficult for me to get another one. In my world, the world of ideas, research, and public service of various kinds, sacrificing intellectual independence to funder pressure is a betrayal of our deepest values.

Disgrace and self-doubt go hand in hand. I began to ask myself whether I really was a leader, or at least whether I was a good one. I often give talks on leadership, and always make the point, particularly to audiences of young women, that I did not think of myself as a leader until my late thirties, and then only after my husband prompted me to put myself up for the presidency of the leading professional organization in my field. Still, for the past twenty-odd years, being a leader has become an important part of my identity—as an executive, author, teacher, mentor, and parent. Now, however, friends and even some family members were gently suggesting that perhaps my true strength lay more in thought leadership than organizational leadership.

Lying there in the dark, I also had to confront the possibility that this crisis was part of a pattern. As I will relate, I had had a number of knocks over the previous six or seven years, expectations dashed and revelations of the ways others thought and talked about me that were far from the way I saw myself. That gap is true of almost everyone, of course—people talk behind our backs. It is just that in the age of leaked emails and social media, we are more likely to be confronted with it.

The criticisms or judgments of others may be motivated by jealousy, or spite, or the simple human desire to be part of an in-group by making others part of the out-group. They may be the product of deep bias—racial, gender, class, and other sources of difference—in which case the task is to push back hard and not allow them to undermine often fragile self-esteem. Still, finding out what others truly think of us, based on their words and actions, can be a mirror that some of us, at least, need the courage to look into. *Why* is what we see—so shaped by what we want to see and what we allow ourselves to see—so different from what others apparently see? I was preparing to find out.

Facing that gap between what we see and what others see is the path to growth—for people but also nations. I often think about this moment in American history as one in which the white majority must work hard to hear and accept the very different narratives of our past that minority communities have experienced and long shared among themselves. As a white woman who grew up in Charlottesville, Virginia, the home of Thomas Jefferson, I grew up with the soaring stories of the Declaration of Independence and the group of Virginians (Washington, Jefferson, Madison, Monroe, and many others) who founded and shaped the early Republic in the image of universal ideals of human liberty, equality, and justice. I toured Monticello many times on school trips and family visits, learning about Jefferson the architect, inventor, botanist, lawyer, diplomat, politician, correspondent, educator, philosopher. Never about Jefferson the slaveholder.

Moreover, like many white Americans, until a few years ago I had never read Frederick Douglass's Fourth of July address from 1852, "What to the Slave Is the Fourth of July?"[1] He addressed his audience, the Ladies' Anti-Slavery Society in Rochester, New York, as "fellow citizens," but of a different nation. The Fourth of July, he said, "is the birthday of your National Independence, and of your political freedom. This, to you, is what the Passover was to the emancipated people of God. It carries your minds back to the day, and to the act of your great deliverance; and to the signs, and to the wonders, associated with that act, and that day." He described the events of 1776 in the most stirring possible terms, of a revolt for freedom against tyranny, justice against injustice. He called the Declaration of Independence "the ring-bolt to the chain of your nation's destiny," a document setting forth principles that Americans should stand by for all eternity. He praised the founding fathers as deeply and fulsomely as generations of Fourth of July orators ever have.

In short, Douglass painted exactly the picture of the glorious past that so many white Americans see when we look in the historical mirror. But then he turned, insisting that his audience look more closely into that mirror to see what so many Americans refused and still refuse to see. He told his audience the story that African Americans, and indeed many people around the world, repeated behind their backs. The story of two Americas.

The rich inheritance of justice, liberty, prosperity and independence, bequeathed by our fathers, is shared by you, not by me. The sunlight that brought life and healing to you, has brought stripes and death to me. This Fourth [of] July is yours, not mine. You may rejoice, I must mourn. To drag a man in fetters into the grand illuminated temple of liberty, and call upon him to join you in joyous anthems, were inhuman mockery and sacrilegious irony. Do you mean, citizens, to mock me, by asking me to speak to-day?

Reading that speech should become as much of a Fourth of July ritual as fireworks, to mark a day of reflection and recognition as much as celebration.

Over the course of my lifetime, scholars, journalists, and activists have started to close the gap between those two Americas. During the Bicentennial Celebration in 1976, the *New York Times* ran a story on Jefferson's descendants, tracing them through the generations and across the country. The article mentioned allegations "through the years" that "the Jefferson family includes descendants of Sally Hemings, a Monticello slave who was reportedly Jefferson's mistress," something I had never heard growing up and certainly not mentioned at Monticello.[2] Some two decades later, historian Annette Gordon Reed published *Thomas Jefferson and Sally Hemings: An American Controversy*, documenting the overwhelming likelihood that Sally Hemings was Jefferson's enslaved concubine, as their son Madison Hemings described her, as well as his wife's half-sister.[3]

Today, Monticello is a very different place. Visitors still enter the elegant hall with moose and elk antlers sent back by Lewis and Clark mounted on the wall, a Native American buffalo robe overhanging the balcony, and marble busts of Voltaire and Alexander Hamilton flanking the entranceway. They still admire the dumbwaiter and the copy desk of Jefferson's invention and marvel at the views of the Blue Ridge mountains through the French windows. They hear that Jefferson wanted to be remembered, not as president or secretary of state, but as "Author of the Declaration of American Independence, of the Statute of Virginia for Religious Freedom, and Father of the University of Virginia."

Yet at every turn, the tour guides also tell the stories of the enslaved people who made Monticello, and indeed Jefferson's entire career and lifestyle, possible. Visitors hear about Sally Hemings, and learn that she and her children with Jefferson remained enslaved, although he freed them before or at his death.[4] They see reconstructions of the small cabins of Mulberry Row, where those men, women, and children lived and worked, practicing the trades necessary for the plantation to function, not only without payment but as property themselves. As Hamilton puts it in his "cabinet battle" against Jefferson in Lin-Manuel Miranda's musical *Hamilton*: "A civics lesson from a slaver, hey neighbor, your debts are paid cuz you don't pay for labor."[5]

Many visitors don't like this new approach. They want to venerate Jefferson, and indeed the entire American founding, without disturbance or discomfort. As one woman said when hearing about how enslaved people planted and tended Monticello's gardens, "Why are you talking about that? You should be talking about the plants."[6]

Douglass expected that resistance. His Fourth of July address is long and rarely read in its entirety. Its descriptions of slavery are brutal and unsparing, his denunciation of the complicity of American churches merciless, and his comparison of the United States with all the nations of the earth concludes that "for revolting barbarity and shameless hypocrisy, America reigns without a rival."

Still, in his conclusion, Douglass finds hope, "drawing encouragement from the Declaration of Independence, the great principles it contains, and the genius of American institutions." He also believes that knowledge matters, that exposing evil to the "all-pervading light" of the world will hasten its downfall.

Do we, as a nation, have the courage to look in the mirror, past and present, as honestly as possible? To hear and accept at least some of what others say about us—our fellow citizens and the people of other countries who see us from the outside in? Yet can we also do that while maintaining enough pride and confidence in ourselves to move forward? To renew our ideals and recommit to being our best selves without hiding from our worst deeds and impulses? Can we undertake this quest while remembering that "we" must contain multitudes? Our national motto is *e pluribus unum*: "Out of many, one." Going forward, can we find a way to be *plures* (the correct Latin form of *pluribus* when used this way) and *unum* at the same time?

As the weeks and months marched on, New America began to right the ship, with other members of the leadership team stepping up and staff members rallying around a new mission statement and an even higher set of standards for transparency and integrity for future funding. That mission statement commits us to "renewing the promise of America by continuing the quest to realize our nation's highest ideals."

Why renewal and not reinvention or restoration? Renewal means to "make new, fresh, or strong again,"[7] a concept that looks backward and forward at the same time. *Renew; Renew.* The "re" is a constant returning, to our past but also to our ideals; the "new" is creating something that has not existed before.[8]

Reinvention starts fresh, while renewal begins with something already there. Some parts of what is there must be rejected, but other parts can be celebrated. Renewal will require Americans to figure out what we can be proud of as well as what we must condemn and repent.

Restoration, on the other hand, is something very different: an effort to turn back the clock. To achieve the energy and power of renewal requires profound change. In *The Fire Next Time*, James Baldwin writes of the need both "to celebrate what is constant" and "to be able and willing to change." "I speak of change not on the surface but in the depths," he continues, "change in the sense of renewal."[9]

Our Constitution has survived by changing with the times, through formal and informal amendments and ongoing judicial interpretation. Yet the distinction between restoration, reinvention, and renewal lies at the crux of many judicial battles. Some judges and legal scholars, who call themselves "originalists," want to pin us down to a specific interpretation of a word or clause held hundreds of years ago by propertied white men in a deeply racist, sexist, and classist age. Others, often labeled as "judicial activists" on both the left and the right, would reinvent the rules that govern us according to contemporary political need. Renewal is in between, constrained by the text in the absence of the national political will to amend it but offering a new understanding of that text by applying the soaring words and universal vision set forth in the Preamble, the Declaration of Independence, and other founding documents to a very different America.

Renewal is also different from renovation, a distinction that has taken me a long time to appreciate. When I would talk about "renewing America" at staff meetings at New America, many of my colleagues heard something that sounded like "making America great again," a phrase and concept that ignores the many ways in which our past was most definitely *not* great for many Americans. I would explain that my concept of renewal was very different, that it was like ripping out the parts of a house or building that were outdated, ugly, or dangerous but keeping the parts that had beauty and strength: the foundation, the frame, old walls and moldings,

the original wood floors. Many towns and cities across America
are doing just that: abandoning twentieth-century malls and
rediscovering their nineteenth-century downtowns, renovating
them physically and finding new uses for old spaces. Banks become restaurants; movie theaters become meeting halls or
makerspaces; shops become galleries.[10]

We needed to renew the country the same way, I would say.
Keep the frame and the foundation (we call the drafters of the
Constitution "framers," after all), accept good parts of our history,
but find, face, and rip out the outdated, ugly, and dangerous
parts. Yet I have come to understand why that concept of renewal
will not serve. We can't just rip out the parts of our past that we
regret and consign them to the historical dumpster. We must
keep them nearby, creating new monuments and memorials
that remind us of what we have done and must never do again.

Moreover, many of the country's cracks and flaws were built
into the foundation. Facing them, and their continuing legacy,
is a task of reflection and restitution, not destruction. We can
renew our commitment to a better future by recommitting to
our highest national ideals and striving to realize them, but we
cannot erase our past or our present.

Renewal often has a spiritual dimension; it is a concept that
recurs in many religious texts. To achieve change on the scale
we need requires an element of faith, a belief that it can happen
without always being able to see how. True national renewal
will require that Americans, *all* Americans, affirm a civic cove-
nant to make the great principles of the Declaration of Independence real and universal. To affirm and renew a civic faith.

No one person could ever represent the nation, much less provide a template for national behavior. Yet individual experience

can provide new analogies and fresh lenses for thinking about and seeing the nation. Personal transformation can also inspire others.

In other ways, what we do in our lives can have direct bearing on what we do in our workplaces, communities, and countries. The "nation," after all, is not some abstract thing floating out there; it is all of us. We must see ourselves differently if we are truly to see our country differently.

I was well into writing this book when a friend circulated a speech by John Gardner—legendary public servant, entrepreneur, leader, teacher, writer, and founder of the progressive political reform group Common Cause—on "personal renewal."[11] Gardner believed that personal renewal was the answer to going stale in midlife: a way of remaining vital, engaged, and curious throughout our lives, continually discovering new possibilities and new potentials within ourselves. He gave this speech in 1990, but it turns out that he had written a book nearly thirty years earlier called *Self-Renewal: The Individual and the Innovative Society*, arguing that a society could not renew itself unless it produces "men and women with the capacity for self-renewal."[12]

Gardner's vision of a vital, innovative, perpetually self-renewing society full of vital, innovative, perpetually self-renewing individuals is compelling, and very American. He was writing at a time when he could look around and see both the energy of Kennedy's race for the moon and what he saw as the "apathy," "rigidity," and "moral emptiness" of much of the rest of American society.[13] Sixty years on, however, I think the most fundamental connection between personal and national renewal is a starker, harder one. The "re" in renewal, the looking back, cannot be avoided.

Writing about the nation's need to confront 250 years of slavery, author Isabelle Wilkerson also analogizes between the individual and the nation. "In the same way that individuals cannot move forward, become whole and healthy, unless they examine the domestic violence they witnessed as children or the alcoholism that runs in their family," she writes, "the country cannot become whole until it confronts what was not a chapter in its history, but the basis of its economic and social order."[14] The country, once again, is the people. Becoming whole requires at least a majority of Americans to see our past, including many of our own ancestors, differently. Not to blame, and thereby to shift responsibility, so much as to face and condemn. And to understand that we cannot tell the bright, happy stories without the dark, painful ones woven in.

This link is both personal and institutional, a lesson I learned in the turbulent summer of 2020.

George Floyd was murdered by Minneapolis police officer Derek Chauvin on May 25, 2020, following the murder of Ahmaud Arbery, a jogger gunned down by white vigilantes in February, and the criminally negligent homicide of Breonna Taylor by Louisville police officers in March. Their deaths followed in the wake of so many others, but this time they came as Black, Hispanic, and Indigenous Americans were dying disproportionately from the COVID-19 pandemic, due to the underlying disparities in health, health care, nutrition, housing, education, and wealth that result from systemic racism. Americans locked down at home, and indeed people around the world, also could not look away from a chilling nine-minute video showing a callous and brutal indifference to Black life. Multiracial crowds poured into the streets to demand racial and social justice, month after month.

In June, many corporations and organizations began issuing statements condemning systemic racism. I began working with

Tyra Mariani, then my president and COO at New America and a woman you will hear more about, on our statement. As we were drafting, Tyra said that she was quite certain she knew how African American employees and other employees of color at our fellow think tanks were reacting to the statements being put out by their leadership. All of those statements were condemning systemic racism "out there," a disembodied harm floating through society, she said, but what about the racism "in here," shaping our institutions and ourselves?

I did not realize that Tyra's point was widespread and obvious in the Black community, and presumably in other communities of color, so much so that cultural critic Soraya McDonald refers to it as "TROT," "Those Racists Over There," a "figment of white imagination and absolution" designed to avoid reckoning with "The Problem We All Live With."[15] The point is simple. There will be no change out there, with regard to systemic racism or a host of other national and global problems, without real change in here, in ourselves and in how we relate to one another in our families, organizations, and communities. The process of renewal, with its double movement backward and forward, offers a path to that change.

In the chapters that follow, I will relate the stages of my own renewal and offer lessons and lenses on resilience, risk, leadership, and power. I will also introduce you to concepts and authors I have discovered in my research, an eclectic but connected group.

We start in chapter 1 with "running toward the criticism," perhaps the single most valuable lesson I have learned over the past decade. Chapter 2 turns to a concept of resilience much broader than I had previously understood, a capacity that is not some innate trait but rather a collective state. Chapter 3 explores a new way of thinking about risk, one that led me to assess my own past and, indeed, myself quite differently, and to contemplate very different prescriptions to encourage risk-taking nationwide. In chapters 4 and 5, I turn more to my experiences as a CEO, reflecting on changes I have made (or am making in what is inevitably an ongoing process) in how I lead and exercise power. In each of these chapters, I try to imagine what applying these precepts or perspectives nationally might look like.

Chapter 6 pauses to review and reflect on the first part of the journey, to return to the broad concept of renewal, and to introduce the second half of the book. Chapters 7, 8, 9, and 10 grapple with larger themes of American renewal: history, identity, transformation, and spirituality. My own experiences inform these explorations, as they must, but in a spirit not of crisis but of hope.

What if we start to believe again that we are capable of great things as a nation, a nation that reflects all the people of the world, including the indigenous people who were on the northern and southern continents in the Western hemisphere long before any Europeans arrived, and yet is distinctively American? What should we be, could we be, in 2076, at the nation's three hundredth anniversary? Novelist Omar Akkad has a deeply dystopian but plausible vision of a second Civil War breaking out in 2074.[16] What are our *utopias*? We have to at least be able to imagine them.

I am guided all the way through by the Langston Hughes poem that is the epigraph: describing a country of hypocrisy, possibility, and conviction, one "that has never been yet, yet must be." Only if we believe and act on the truth, apparently not so self-evident after all, that all human beings are created equal.

A final note. I have imagined many audiences while writing this book, but I hope women will pay particular attention. Women have a particular role to play in this moment in American and world history, just as we have had at key moments in the past: the abolitionists, the suffragettes, the Woman's Christian Temperance Union movement, the settlement house movement, the muckrakers, the civil rights movement, the environmental movement, and of course the multiple waves of the current women's movement. Women were either the principal players or key players in all of those movements, even as their contributions were often ignored or pushed aside by men and as white women dismissed and denigrated women of color.[17] Today, we have Me Too, the National Domestic Women's Alliance, and the Black Lives Matter Global Network, all of which were founded by women.

As Rebecca Traister writes, women in the United States "have never been taught how noncompliant, insistent, furious women have shaped our history and our present, our activism and our art. We should be."[18] On the contrary, female anger, particularly for Black women, is derided and dismissed. Brittney Cooper expresses both her underlying rage and her anger at the ways in which it is typically treated: "Angry Black Women get dismissed all the time. . . . The story goes that Angry Black Women scare babies, old people, and grown men. This is absurd. And it is a lie."[19]

Yet anger need not be feared. "Redemptive anger," according to social justice activist Ruby Sales, is "the anger that . . . moves you to transformation and human up-building." It fuels the energy and determination necessary to make change happen.[20] It is the antidote to apathy and despair.

Women can also unite through the experience of multiple identities. We are different from one another in so many ways, ways that are critical to recognize. The women of the Combahee River Collective, for instance, issued a statement defining and describing Black feminism in 1977 (they named their collective for a daring raid led by Harriet Tubman in 1863). "No one before," they wrote, "has ever examined the multilayered texture of Black women's lives," what legal scholar Kimberle Crenshaw described a decade later as the intersectionality of race and gender, as well as other identities.[21] As we will see, much of Black feminism has been defined against the insularity and racism of white feminism, a divide almost two centuries old. That example is only one of the many different ways women hurt, exclude, dominate, and dismiss one another.

Still, all women—all American women and women everywhere—have had the experience of being defined *only* in relationship to others—as mother, daughter, sister, wife. Many of us cherish those identities, yet they all too often mean that we have not been seen as fully human authors of our own lives. We have fought—are still fighting—to be recognized for our own goals, achievements, and needs.

That common experience can be a bridge, even if it is sometimes a slender span over a wide river. It can help us lead others to an understanding of what true pluralism can mean, embracing many different identities at once as individuals and as a country. It can, I hope, help us bring together the many different movements we support and lead in a common quest for renewal.

CHAPTER 1

Run toward the Criticism

As the crisis at New America unfolded, I spent days on the phone with staff members and board members. One of the first people I called was my friend and mentor David Bradley, the chairman of Atlantic Media, who had run New America's search for a new leader back in 2012 and was more responsible than anyone for persuading me to take the job.

David is a superb mentor to a remarkable array of people. He seeks out young people in whom he sees some quality and brings them into his orbit, offering hard-earned wisdom and insights from a lifetime of entrepreneurship and service of many different kinds. He did not mince words when I called him—in his capacity as friend and guide as much as New America board member. We both knew I was in trouble.

He said: "run toward the criticism." Even if you are 98 percent right and only 2 percent wrong, he elaborated, acknowledge the fault rather than insist on the virtue. Then use it as the point of departure for a "learning journey." A journey in which I would deliberately ask for honest critique, even if deep down I wanted to run as fast as possible in the other direction.

I therefore called the twenty-odd other board members and asked each one to tell me directly what they truly thought of my leadership. Having sat on many boards myself, and as a lawyer, I well understand the difference between friendship and fiduciary duty. It is possible to like a CEO and even believe that she has done the best she could under the circumstances, and still believe that she must be censured or fired for the good of the organization. I was closer to some board members than others, so my heart was often pounding as I dialed, but the process itself drew us together. I can still remember a number of those conversations and the insights I gained, even if some made me wince.

My colleagues, junior and senior, were also willing to be honest. Not everyone had the courage to say to my face what I had reason to suspect they were saying behind my back. Still, I heard some hard truths. The board hired a consultant to interview staff members about both the incident that led to the crisis and the possibility of deeper trouble in the organization. The resulting report was studded with quotes from staff members—all anonymous, of course—some of which described a very different New America from the one I thought I led.

Some of what I heard I already knew. I was not in the office enough—because I was on the road fundraising and flying the New America flag publicly, but also because I still live in Princeton and was commuting to DC only a few days a week. I moved too fast and didn't consult enough. I didn't spend enough time getting to know staff members and their work; I communicated too much through email and not enough in person.

I also heard things that I did not expect, and that took me longer to accept. I was in regular contact with Hana Passen, a young woman whom I had hired right out of college and then promoted to a bigger position at New America after three years. I am her mentor, but in many ways she has mentored me as well—particularly on issues of race and social justice. Even as she had faith in me—in my intentions, my track record, and my leadership—Hana let me know that others at New America were far less willing to give me the benefit of the doubt with regard to corporate influence, favoritism, double standards, and insensitivity.

As Hana put it, even if my staff—particularly younger staff—did not exactly think I was lying, they also didn't necessarily trust me. Earlier missteps and sore spots were quickly raised again, reinforcing negative perceptions of my leadership and New America's culture more generally.

Looking back, I can see that many of the issues raised tap into the intergenerational differences that so many boomer bosses complain about with largely millennial workforces. We are unprepared, unsure, and often uncomfortable trying to manage a younger generation that is more radical, demanding, and impatient for change. While I naively assumed that my good intentions were both apparent and sufficient, many New America staff wanted far more action on issues of race, gender, and class. Perhaps also reflecting the dramatic trust gaps in the country as a whole, many staff members quickly defaulted to distrust in their perceptions of me, just as, if I'm honest, I did in my perceptions of them.

In short, if I chose to run toward the criticism, I didn't have to look very far. I know now that those were the first steps toward renewal.

━━━

Renewal starts with honesty—radical honesty. It was time to let down defenses, to start acknowledging things that I knew to be true and exploring things that might be. This process was partly a version of the therapist's mantra: "you have to name it to change it." Yet not everything can be "fixed." Behaviors can change, with a lot of work; personality traits, not so much.[1] Still, it is surely better to face yourself honestly, even if all you can do is sit with the truth.

More concretely, "running toward the criticism" required that I widen my perspective, look beyond the present situation to earlier parts of my career. I needed to identify and face up to a larger pattern of cause and consequence, as honestly as I could. Even the most successful people have had setbacks and failures; the question should always be "what can I learn?"

As dean of Princeton's School of Public and International Affairs from 2002 to 2009, I could point to many achievements of which I will always be proud. I recruited an entire group of top-notch international relations scholars and increased the size of the faculty as a whole by nearly one-third. These new faculty members largely came from other Princeton departments: I added experts in history, sociology, engineering, and the natural sciences to broaden the school's focus away from pure economics and political science. I worked with faculty members to launch a number of centers and programs, most notably the Scholars in the Nation's Service Initiative, a kind of Rhodes Scholarship for students who wanted to work in the federal government. The school's public profile increased even as we defended successfully against a nasty and hugely time-consuming lawsuit. I upgraded school facilities and raised the morale of the administrative staff by valuing their contributions in an environment in which faculty and students typically get all the attention.

My successor as dean, Christina Paxson, was a talented and far-sighted economist who had founded the school's Center for Health and Wellbeing. Only a few years into her tenure, she was tapped to become the president of Brown University, where she has been very successful. As she left unexpectedly, Princeton University's then-president Shirley Tilghman needed to appoint an interim dean for a year to allow the school to run a proper search for Chris's successor. Princeton's typical practice in these circumstances, when a former dean has returned to the faculty, is to appoint him or her as interim dean.

I waited for the call. It didn't come. When I went to President Tilghman to offer my services, she demurred. She had hired me in 2002, in the face of a fair amount of faculty opposition, and had been a friend, mentor, and champion during my deanship, but something had changed. When I pressed for an explanation, she essentially told me that a block of the faculty would object to my appointment as interim dean—effectively a vote of no confidence.

Looking back, given the perpetual power games of faculty politics and the opposition to my appointment in the first place, I probably should not have been surprised. I was hardly dying to be interim dean for a year, but the episode made me think about what I really did want for the next stage of my career. After three decades of focusing on foreign affairs, I was beginning to see that if the United States could not fix its mounting problems at home, it had no business trying to lead the world. I had fallen in love with civic technology and its promise of dramatically improved government services. Many new opportunities were also opening up in my life as a result of my unexpected prominence as a participant in rekindled debates about gender equality. I put academia behind me and took on the challenges of leading and building New America.

In the fall of 2017, however, when I once again realized that in the face of a major challenge to my leadership, I could not exactly point to a groundswell of support from those I led, I had to put the two episodes together and ask myself hard questions. Or, rather, ask others. I went back to Shirley, now retired, and invited her to be as honest as she could be about my flaws as a leader.

She told me, in essence, that I had put myself forward too much, which also meant not putting others forward enough. I had a tremendously talented group of faculty members, including Nobel laureates and scholars doing important work on a wide range of subjects: climate change, poverty, immigration, family policy, trade, corruption, and many others. I missed opportunities to let them shine, and, equally important, to feel that they were part of deciding the direction of the school.

As I listened to her, I could hear echoes of the critiques I had gotten while talking to board and staff members at New America. I could also feel lots of counterarguments forming in my mind. Shirley had hired me to transform the school in a number of ways; it is almost impossible to do that without making enemies—or so I thought. I had hired and empowered many different faculty members to do the work they wanted to do; I had created opportunities for them to publicize their work that they didn't take. Et cetera, et cetera.

Above all, I kept wondering whether I would have been subject to the same criticisms had I been a man. The double standards for women leaders—in every sector—are legion. When we are decisive, we have "sharp elbows." When we are prominent, we are "hogging the limelight." When we earn big salaries (almost always still far less than men in comparable positions), we are greedy. Any woman leader can add to this list.

We also get mixed messages. While we are often very ready to step forward and take responsibility for our actions, vowing to do better, we hear the voices of men in our lives telling us to project certainty and confidence, to lead the way so many men traditionally have. Indeed, according to one leadership study, men *and* women prefer stereotypically masculine traits in leaders (confidence, ambition, competitiveness, assertiveness, decisiveness, and self-reliance) to stereotypically feminine traits (cooperation, good nature, trustworthiness, tolerance, sincerity, patience). And yet as every woman leader knows all too well, female confidence is still far too often read as unattractive egotism.[2]

Even as these thoughts were running through my mind, however, I was also reminding myself that Shirley was one of the best leaders I had ever seen. When she stepped down as president of Princeton, she was universally beloved. Indeed, in all the time I worked for her, I didn't know anyone who really disliked her, even when they disagreed with her decisions. Yet, she had managed to transform the university in many different ways over her twelve-year tenure. I also thought of another mentor of mine, Nannerl Keohane, president of Wellesley College and then the first woman president of Duke, who led in much the same way. They both took the time and effort to build relationships even with those who opposed them, tempering professional tensions with personal connections.

As I have reflected on this conversation over the past couple of years, I also think back on an incident when Shirley and I traveled to meet a group of Princeton alumni on Capitol Hill. Shirley introduced me as the new dean of the Woodrow Wilson School (now the Princeton School of Public and International Affairs); I talked for a while and got an overwhelmingly positive reception. Afterward I said to Shirley, "I didn't mean to steal your thunder." She said, without missing a beat, "Anne-Marie, you *are* my thunder," and often told the story to alumni groups after that. As it turned out, I proved less adept at letting other people be *my* thunder, something I could choose to change.

In the end, the balance of praise and criticism doesn't matter. David Bradley's wisdom is not just to run toward the things you don't want to hear; it is to run toward them even if they are only 2 percent right and 98 percent wrong. Accept that 2, or 10, or 50 percent and embrace it as a catalyst for change.

The danger of radical honesty, at least for me, was the risk of losing my confidence. I depend on a measure of confidence to do the things I do every day, from running meetings to giving speeches. One example will tell the tale.

I make my living in part as a public speaker; I speak to large audiences for up to an hour, usually without notes. Yet I was absolutely terrified of public speaking until my mid to late thirties. In law school, I chose corporate law over litigation because I couldn't imagine having to stand up in court. The night before I taught my first class at the University of Chicago Law School, I went to the empty classroom and practiced my opening lines for an hour, out of fear that I would get up in front of the class the next day and simply be unable to speak. When I had to sit on a panel at conferences or give a speech, I typically read from a text and my voice often shook.

I tell this story often, particularly when I am talking to groups of young women. I tell them that they simply have to put themselves out there; force themselves up on stage and speak enough that they begin to realize they can do it. As I began to get more invitations to speak, I gradually realized that speaking from a text or even detailed notes was a problem, because I would look up and ad lib for a while and then lose my place when I looked back down. I realized that in private conversation, as my brother would say, "I have no problem with word retrieval." So, if I know what I want to say, why should it be any different in front of an audience? I began to speak from fewer notes, just a few points jotted down, and then from no notes at all.

Having confidence made all the difference. Confidence is an elixir, a magic well that you can draw from again and again. I began to realize that I could stand up in front of any number of people and engage them, move them, inspire them—that confidence flowed from me to the audience and back. Moreover, confidence is absolutely indispensable for a leader, although the line between confidence and hubris is thin and easily crossed. More about that later. But if you do not have confidence in yourself, others will not have confidence in you—at least those you are supposed to be leading. (Parents, mentors, and managers are different—their job is to have confidence in you when you don't always have it in yourself.)

Confidence is even more important for a woman. Journalists Katty Kay and Claire Shipman argue that lack of confidence is the key reason that men are still so far ahead of women in the corporate and political worlds.[3] I work out on a stationary bike with instructors urging me on over a video screen; one of my favorite male instructors tells the class that pushing through is all a matter of confidence, which he says the men in the class will of course "get," but the women will have a harder time.

We could spend a long time dissecting the reasons that women doubt themselves more than men do, as well as exploring the ways in which different categories of women experience multiple layers of social rejection. Women of color must combat the cancer of creeping self-doubt even more than similarly situated white women, as Michelle Obama attests in *Becoming*.[4] Indeed, when my colleague Cecilia Muñoz wrote an account of her own "becoming," she titled it *More than Ready*, a play on the idea that women of color are both more than ready to take their place at the table in our society and when they finally get to the table they are more ready than they need to be because they overprepare for everything.[5] Working twice as hard (to get half as far, a frequent saying in communities of color) is one way to build confidence.

It is thus not surprising that one of the ways I gained confidence in my thirties and forties was by learning from the men in my life. My husband would periodically point out that I had undermined myself by beginning a remark with, "I'm not an expert, but I think . . ."—classic feminine self-deprecation. "If you start by telling people you are not an expert," he would say, "why should anyone listen to the rest of your sentence?" I took cues from him and the many other men in my professional life on how to present myself, projecting strength and competence through both body language and a loud, authoritative voice. I gradually came to see myself not only as a leader but also as a builder and a bulwark whom others could rely on.

I could not afford now to go back to that far shakier younger self. I could, however, begin to question whether the male display of overt confidence that I had absorbed was the only way. I could read Brené Brown on vulnerability and leadership;[6] I could explore the idea that much of what I had mistaken for confidence in many men might often be bluster and swagger to hide insecurity. I could begin to imagine a new confidence based on critical self-reflection—running toward the criticism—as a practice for internal transformation.[7]

━━━━━

What would that take for you? For all of us? How does each of us shut off the rationalizing voices that offer up excuses and explanations for our actions, putting up a defensive stockade? Remember, national renewal will also require individual renewal—a critical mass of people finding the courage and commitment to make real change in how we assess ourselves and relate to others. Evidence of that transformation pops up in some surprising places.

Some of the bravest self-exploration I have read comes from memoirs by African American men: men who grew up with the world stacked against them, with lives indelibly stamped by race, class, geography, violence, and difference. They are men who know what it is, as activist Darnell Moore puts it, to exist "on the edges of the margins."[8] They are Black men who write about being fat, gay, alcoholic, addicted. They each tell stories of struggling with self-hatred and finding refuge in drugs, booze, food, gambling, or flight.[9]

These men have plenty of reasons to rationalize their failings, or simply to hide from them. Yet each made his way back to sanity and community by facing himself and his past: the deep complexities of family life, including love-hate relationships with parents and siblings; the ugliness and pain of violence received and inflicted; the efforts to escape or submerge feelings of guilt, inadequacy, rage, and fear. As the reader, I experience the honesty and pain flowing through the pages as an act of catharsis, a path back to love and grace.

At the end of his memoir *Heavy*, writer and professor Kiese Laymon tells his mother, who wants him to have a child: "We cannot responsibly love anyone, and especially not black children in America, if we insist on making a practice of hiding and running from ourselves." When she asks him to promise he will change his life, he remembers that "the most abusive parts of our nation obsessively neglect yesterday while peddling in possibility," that "we got here by refusing to honestly remember together," that it is easier to promise than to reckon and change.[10]

If Americans, or indeed any people who would prefer to bury parts of their past, *were* "to honestly remember together," what would that look like? We have one example already. Putting a National Museum of African American History and Culture near the center of the National Mall, just steps from the Washington Monument, invites all Americans and all visitors to the United States to experience a very different facet of U.S. history than the account traditionally presented at the National Museum of American History, which I remember visiting regularly on school and family trips as a child. We would enter a grand hall featuring the original star-spangled banner, the actual flag, tattered now, that flew over the ramparts at the Battle of Baltimore and inspired Francis Scott Key to write the national anthem.

Visitors to the African American History museum enter a lobby full of light and art, but then begin their tour by descending several floors to a cramped, low-ceilinged, dimly lit space that simulates the hold of a slave ship crossing the Atlantic in the infamous "Middle Passage." "Middle" because it was the middle leg of the triangular journey that began with European traders sailing to West Africa to exchange manufactured goods for human cargo—enslaved men, women, and children—whom they then delivered to the West Indies and sold in return for rice, sugar, and tobacco, which they took back to Europe. All North, South, and Central Americans other than those descended from indigenous peoples can ultimately trace their arrival in the Western hemisphere back to a sea journey, but none as brutal as this one. For the millions of Africans who were forced into exile in the United States, it was the beginning of centuries of dehumanization.

Running toward the criticism, as a nation, means embracing this history—all of this history—as *our* American history. It means honoring neglected or suppressed parts of our history with their own museums and monuments, as the Equal Justice Initiative, led by public interest lawyer Bryan Stevenson, has done so powerfully with the National Memorial for Peace and Justice in Montgomery, Alabama.[11] The memorial names and remembers thousands of Black Americans who were lynched over decades of terror in the South, strung up and often burned or mutilated, by vigilante mobs. It is modeled on memorials to the Holocaust in Berlin and to apartheid in South Africa, inviting comparison and reflection.

Running toward the criticism also means updating older buildings and exhibits to be far more accurate and inclusive, as we have seen with Monticello and also with the National Museum of American History, which now tells the history of the civil rights movement not as African American history but as *American* history. For all of us, it means reading as widely as we can and reflecting on our own ancestors, whoever they may be, and on their role in shaping the nation we are today—for both good and evil. Don't flinch or hide.

Remember also, however, that the criticism, no matter how searing, is never the whole story, any more than the praise is. The star-spangled banner is still displayed in the American history museum, now with an entire exhibit room dedicated to preserving the fragile cloth and exploring its history, including Key's veneration of the "land of the free" when he was a slaveholder. He was a hypocrite and certainly a racist by today's standards, and even by the standards of many of his contemporaries. Yet he also wrote the soaring national anthem that most Americans sing with our hands over our hearts, about a flag that Americans of all races, creeds, and ethnicities have fought for even as they questioned what it stood for.

Here is the central tension of renewal. Self-hatred and pervasive shame is toxic and counterproductive, for individuals, communities, or countries. I can find many things in American history to be proud of, beginning with the language and principles of the Declaration and a set of institutions, as radically imperfect as they are, that have allowed a steady widening of the circles of inclusion. But I have also come to understand the danger, pain, and continuing oppression in that progress narrative, and the need for me to give up at least some of the things that I cherish to clear space for other stories and a wider set of less self-serving truths.

Running toward the criticism does not mean obliterating the traditional narrative, but complicating it, just as when you or I absorb personal criticism, we should not let it obliterate the good in us. We try to learn and grow. This practice, of embracing critique, the way an athlete seeks a coach who will push her continually through correction, can help us knit the country back together.

According to journalist Amanda Ripley, "complicating the narrative" is essential to escaping what she identifies as "intractable conflict" or "high conflict": the kind of conflict America is currently experiencing.[12] In these situations, tribal differences become charged in such a way as to create a heightened threat awareness in the brain, which in turn shuts down normal attributes like curiosity or openness to new information. In these "hypervigilant states," facts essentially become irrelevant.[13]

Journalists make these conflicts worse, Ripley argues, by stirring powerful emotions, as they are trained to do to grab a reader's attention, and by giving their publics the tidy coherence they crave. When people are already polarized, however, those emotions fuel ever more toxic reactions and result in dangerous oversimplification. "Complexity collapses, and the us-versus-them narrative sucks the oxygen from the room."[14] We know the tropes: "Republicans are racist rednecks," or "Democrats are precious snowflakes who hate America."

Ripley interviewed a wide range of experts, from psychologists to rabbis, who know how to disrupt toxic narratives and get people to reveal deeper truths. She participated in an exercise designed to bring people with radically different views at least one step closer to seeing one another as fellow human beings rather than monsters. Her conclusion from all this work was to enjoin her fellow journalists to provide information that does not contradict a position so much as add nuance and complexity. Add the details that make it a richer and more accurate story, one that is much harder to simplify. People are far more likely to listen.[15]

A year after the crisis at New America, in September 2018, I read Emily Wilson's new translation of *The Odyssey*.[16] It was an interesting contrast to Robert Fagles's translation,[17] which, in a fit of ambitious parenting, I had read aloud to my young sons when they were roughly four and six. When I wondered what it was exactly that felt different about Wilson's translation, my elder son was the one who got it. "Ma-ahm," he said, in that slightly exasperated but good-humored way that our children have when they think they are explaining the obvious, "The way you know it was translated by a woman is that Athena, Kalypso, and Circe are real characters." And so they are, drawn with as much detail and feeling as Wilson can wring out of Homer's Greek.

It does not take a degree in psychology to explain why I was suddenly fascinated with odysseys, and particularly their female characters, after a year-long odyssey of my own.[18] Odysseus, at least in Fagles's translation, is the "man of twists and turns."[19] (Emily Wilson just describes him as "complicated.")[20] Twisting and turning describes the subtle trickiness of his mind, but also the many circles of his voyage. When he is almost home, he is blown far off course, losing his way and angering the gods time and again, often through the actions of his men, whom he fails to control.

I have come to understand the moral of the story as the impossibility of moving forward without moving backward first, or indeed simultaneously. Moving backward to face our flaws, to remember and include those we have left behind, to remind ourselves that when we have fallen down, we have needed others to pick us up, thereby girding ourselves with enough humility to know that we will not be able to overcome the obstacles of the future alone.

That is not the moral that Odysseus draws from his own travels. He loses almost all his men but still returns home alone as the avenging and godlike king, slaughtering his wife's suitors (and his own serving maids). Indeed, the wiles of Odysseus's mind are rarely given to introspection of any sort. His life is an eternal competition; *The Odyssey* ends with a battle among Ithacans in which Odysseus turns to his son and says, "soon you will have experience of fighting in battle, the true test of worth. You must not shame your father's family; for years we have been known across the world for courage and manliness."[21] That very male measure of a hero has been handed down for centuries.

No longer. *The Odyssey* can be retold from multiple points of view, in different translations and in novels written from the perspective of Circe or Briseis, the priestess taken as a slave girl whom Achilles and Agamemnon fought over.[22] Or perhaps from the perspective of Eurybates, the Black valet whom Odysseus named his favorite servant because Eurybates's "mind matched his."[23] Penelope, Odysseus's wife renowned chiefly for her patience in keeping her suitors at bay as she waits for him, is just as clever and strategic as her husband, but uses different tools to achieve her ends. She also depends much more on her household than he ever depends on his men.

Growing up and through most of my career, I would have told you that I identified far more with Odysseus than with Penelope. I always loved him because he was the smart one—the hero who used his mind more than his muscles. He was also

Athena's favorite, and Athena—a goddess similarly renowned for her brains more than her beauty—was definitely my favorite Greek immortal. Penelope, by contrast, stayed home and excelled at the domestic household arts that I firmly rejected and indeed refused to learn as a girl (I still can't iron or sew).

Now though, I was coming to respect resilience as much as daring, to reflect on the challenges of withstanding as much as winning. I was only beginning, however, to understand the many different facets of resilience, and the ways in which it requires collective rather than individual strength. This was new terrain for me; exploring it was the next leg of my odyssey.

CHAPTER 2

Connect to Change

A few weeks after my conversation with David Bradley, when New America was still in the thick of the crisis, my board chair and I had a difficult conversation about mistakes I had made, such as sending overly dramatic emails, that had made matters worse. We were in a car on our way to a New America event; I no longer remember the exact words we exchanged, but I can still recall looking out at a particular DC intersection, taking in the light and shadows of a September afternoon, and wanting to be anywhere but there.

On arriving at our destination, some twenty minutes later, I had to give a short speech. My job was to greet more than a hundred people and find words of both welcome and inspiration for the opening of a new year of work (New America always thinks of September as "back to school" month). Any upset, or fear, or fragility simply had to be put away. My board chair was impressed by my ability to switch gears so quickly, and later cited the incident at a full board meeting as an example of my resilience.

As I look back now, however, that wasn't resilience as much as endurance, the simple refusal to be broken. Resilience is something quite different, as I and my New America colleagues came to understand. It is less about surviving or even bouncing back so much as bouncing forward, using pain, humiliation, loss, and fear as catalysts for transformative change. That kind of resilience is less an innate character trait than a capacity that can be developed, in a person, organization, or community. Like all capacities, however, it requires resources, in this case reservoirs of both connection and purpose.

If you had asked me four or five years ago to define "resilience," I think I would have said something like "the ability to withstand adversity." The image in my mind would have been a stone or a mountain, battered by wind, ice, rain, and sun, but still standing. I thought of it as essentially synonymous with a kind of solid and stolid strength.

Alternatively, I might have defined resilience as persistence. I have an oval pewter paperweight on my desk that is inscribed with the words: "Never never never give up."[1] The paperweight is a gift from my longtime assistant, Terry Murphy, an adoptive mother who simply refused to be beaten in her years-long quest to rescue her daughter from an orphanage in Romania. The quotation, slightly modified, is from Winston Churchill.

Images of Churchill invoke ideas of staunch Britons during the dark days of the German blitz, with bombs falling nightly on London and other major British cities, of blackout curtains, strict rationing, and daily news of death and loss from the European front. A refusal to surrender to what life brings need not be so dramatic, however. The persistence—a combination of determination and endurance—that Churchill's words capture is the personal mantra of a number of women I know, from Terry to Hillary Clinton, who urged her audience in a speech in 2017: "Resist. Persist. Insist. Enlist."[2]

Endurance and persistence are close kin to, and perhaps even necessary elements of, resilience, but over the past few years, through listening, reading, and personal reckoning, I have come to understand resilience as something bigger. Lesson one came from a coincidental source. In mid-August 2017, just a week or so before trouble hit, I received a request out of the blue to endorse a book titled *Type R: Transformative Resilience for Thriving in a Turbulent World*, by Ama and Stephanie Marston, a mother-daughter duo. I did not know them, but I agreed because I was intrigued by the idea, little realizing how soon I would need it.

The Marstons begin with the observation that we live in a world of constant change and pervasive, unavoidable uncertainty. In such an environment, we must change the way we respond to adversity: recovering or even "bouncing back" is no longer good enough, and may be impossible. Even the idea of character-building through adversity that those of us who are parents continually repeat to our children ("what doesn't kill you makes you stronger") is not enough.

"Transformative resilience" requires a deeper mindset shift. It is to assume that challenges, problems, and failures are the necessary catalysts for creativity, growth, and positive transformation in directions we cannot anticipate or project in advance. Great inventions and innovations in science, technology, art, and popular culture have come from "individuals who evolved as a result of disruption, discomfort, and hardship."[3] Examples include the theory of gravity, the invention of the microcomputer, and works of art ranging from Beethoven's Ninth Symphony to Frida Kahlo's self-portraits, the Beatles' *Sergeant Pepper's Lonely Hearts Club Band* to Eminem's rap.

The Type R mindset is particularly well suited for a world in which we must give up on the idea of equilibrium or steady-state existence, a world of pandemics, extreme weather, and dizzying technological change. The Marstons insist on "letting go of the idea that we will find 'balance' and instead embracing the world's numerous imbalances."[4] This is an idea that mothers—parents—will welcome, as we recognized long ago that the idea of "work-life balance" is an unattainable state designed to make most of us feel as though we are failing most of the time!

In this world of constantly shifting winds and unpredictable waves, we must give up the idea of charting our course and cutting through the water in a boat powered by oars or a motor. The trick instead is to learn to surf or sail, having goals and destinations in mind but being prepared to get there in new ways, or even setting out in new directions by running with the current.

The ideas here may sound like standard self-help jargon of the "face your fears" variety. The "we" here is also deceptive, as it assumes a minimum level of personal resources that millions of people may not have. Yet when I started to think of resilience as the capacity for personal transformation in the face of adversity, I began to be able to use the fear I felt—of loss of job and reputation, personal humiliation, and lasting damage to my organization—as a spur and indeed an opportunity for change.

Lesson two was the realization that resilience is a team sport. It is certainly possible for each of us to develop and strengthen the "grit" muscle in ourselves and in others, as psychologist and best-selling author Angela Duckworth explains.[5] But in the fall of 2017, as in earlier times of crisis, I realized once again that resilience resides as much in the web of personal relationships that support me as in anything inside me. It was in my beloved brother's insistence, against my protestations that I didn't need or want him to come, on driving from New York to Princeton to take me to dinner and stay the night on one particularly dark evening—in every sense—when I was alone in my house. And in the family grapevine that lets everyone know I need some support seemingly within fifteen minutes after I have talked to one family member, bringing a surge of emails, texts, and calls.

To the extent that this kind of resilience can be built, it is about connection and community. After my name appeared in an unflattering light in two back-to-back articles on the front page of the *New York Times*, I quickly came to appreciate many old friends and to discover a number of new ones as supportive emails poured in. People took the time to bolster me emotionally, particularly people who had faced trials of their own, something I now try to remember whenever I see others in the public stocks.

Some wrote to assure me that they had seen a very different side of my character and leadership than the one being presented. Others affirmed their love and friendship. Many told me stories of their own experiences, assuring me that "this too shall pass." And some offered valuable advice. The value of these messages, and the pain of not hearing from some people I had counted as friends, underlined the role of connection—and the danger of disconnection—in building resilience.

Of course, I was hardly alone in experiencing personal and organizational trauma. Many of my closest colleagues at New America shared the pain and the keen sense of injustice. We worked hard together to find things to laugh about, to bolster one another in moments when fatigue and emotion threatened to overwhelm, and to ensure that the experience would help us learn and grow. The irrepressible Meredith Hanley, then our director of development, insisted even years later on referring to the whole affair not as a crisis but as our "media adventure."

This lesson of connection pops up everywhere. I often think of it as a hidden current running through our atomized, fractured twenty-first-century lives, where we are connected to everyone all the time through the Internet, and connected less and less in the ways that matter: face to face, voice to voice, human to human. The COVID-19 pandemic has underlined this paradox in often horrific ways, with dying patients able to say goodbye to loved ones only through a screen held by a stranger. Hugging, holding one another, seeking solace through touch is a deep dimension of being human.

The dark side of the Internet Age, of course, is that connection per se is certainly not an unalloyed good. Lies, mistrust, the exposure and spread of the very worst of human nature all flow through channels of connection. We must pay close attention to who is connected to whom, and how, and to the nature and content of the resulting interaction. An entire body of network science has emerged that can help us develop strategies of both connection and disconnection, as individuals, organizations, and even nations.[6]

Real, human connection can also be the antidote to digital pain. Joshua Geltzer, who served as the senior director for counterterrorism on the National Security Council in the Obama administration and has spent a great deal of time studying digital communication, terrorist recruiting, and the spread of disinformation, has written about the phenomenon of Internet trolls, those people whose greatest delight is to destroy your day. An important part of combating trolls, he argues, is to develop "a sense of self that transcends one's digital profile"—a self that is embedded in real relationships rather than electronically linked to digital friends and followers.[7]

In 2019, New America published a "digital magazine" on resilience, a compilation of podcasts, articles, interviews, and reflections on its various meanings, its value as a strategy for navigating an age of constant change, and the ways in which it can be cultivated and strengthened. I had the luxury of interviewing many people I admired and asking them to explore what resilience has meant in their own lives.

Many concurred with the idea of resilience as connection—to family, friends, community. Over and over again, our authors and interviewees emphasized the need to tether ourselves to other humans who can catch us when we fall or extend a hand to pull us up. Darren Walker, president of the Ford Foundation, took this point one step further, focusing on the way that even imagined connections can provide an ongoing flow of belief and confidence.

Darren described the many government programs that helped him to grow and learn—from Head Start as a prekindergartener to Pell grants in college—as a continuing testament to his country's cheering him on. The availability of government support, in his view, meant that his fellow Americans believed he was worth investing in, even with their precious tax dollars. Today, he worries that too many children do not feel that "America is cheering them on," investing in their future, and helping them to get back up when they stumble and fall.

That flow of belief and confidence can and should run from citizens and taxpayers to their government as much as from government back to them, as well as from individuals and institutions to one another. That connection is much stronger, however, when it links people in the service of a larger whole, enabling them to understand themselves as the builders of something that will far outlast them, like the builders of a medieval cathedral. This is the terrain on which individual resilience and social resilience begin to merge. In Darren's words, "the commitment to We makes I stronger."

The commitment to "We" makes us stronger still when the glue connecting us is not simply a joint task, but a commitment to a higher purpose. Historian Noah Yuval Harari argues that members of *Homo sapiens* first distinguished themselves as a species some thirty thousand years ago when they began to create art; when they proved themselves capable of imagining something that did not exist in their world.[8] A cause—the abolition of slavery, preserving the environment, a world without poverty, a world with education for all—is a similar exercise in collective imagination, believing in and working for a world that does not exist now but that we can picture in our minds.

Making common cause with our colleagues—coworkers, community members, fellow citizens—is not always easy. We must begin by trying to understand how what is good for one person might have a very disparate impact on another. It is in the very nature of policymaking and the provision of public goods to have to make trade-offs. Blocking the construction of a freeway or new housing on environmental grounds, for instance, could make it harder for people in poorer communities to get to work or afford their rents. Power is also ever present, clothing self-interest or group interest in a veneer of public purpose.

Still, if resilience takes capacity to change and connection to others, joining in a larger cause makes it much easier to put our personal flaws and failures in perspective and even to see them as part of a larger process of inevitable trial and error as the group moves forward and figures out who is best positioned to do what. The interaction of commitment and connection creates a virtuous circle of resilience, where friends and colleagues provide strength and help in overcoming setbacks, all the while deepening a collective commitment to do something bigger and more meaningful than any one of us could do alone.

Cecilia Muñoz teaches me this lesson every day. I first met her in June 2016, when she was still working as the head of the Domestic Policy Council under President Obama, one of the most important jobs in the White House. I was ushered into her office in the West Wing, welcomed by a couple of assistants who reflected the warmth and modesty of her own demeanor (she is a MacArthur genius award winner but you could know her for years without ever finding that out). When I laid out an opportunity to come work at New America, she told me candidly that she was deeply focused on finishing President Obama's domestic agenda in the six to seven months left in his administration and had not yet given a thought to what she would do afterward.

I understood, but told her that I would stay in touch, and began sending regular emails and arranging periodic meetings. We often talked about New America's commitment to public interest technology: the idea, pioneered by organizations like Code for America, that technologists should be aware of and prepare themselves for careers in the public sector as well as the private sector. In our view, these digital whizzes should bring their mindsets and skills to figuring out how to improve public education, ending homelessness, or addressing climate change, as much as how to improve Google's search function or to create the latest app that will make it easier for people to download music or order pizza.

Cecilia was at the center of trying to improve the way all of federal domestic policy works by integrating technology and the technological mindset across the government, working with a corps of talented engineers, product designers, data scientists, and others recruited into the new United States Digital Service. It was hard work; it's certainly possible to design technology to make systems more efficient and effective, but convincing a bureaucrat who is overworked, under continual time pressure, and accustomed to doing things the way they have always been done to actually *use* that technology or incorporate those insights is something else entirely.

Notwithstanding the difficulties, the potential to improve the government's ability both to represent and to serve its citizens is dramatic. Cecilia was deeply interested in continuing that work outside of government. We kept talking about how she might do that at New America, until one fall day, at an early breakfast meeting, she said yes. Explaining what had convinced her, she said something that I will always remember and that I remind myself of from time to time: "I feel called to do this work."

When I interviewed Cecilia years later about her concept of both personal and organizational resilience, she reflected on her long experience working for the National Council of La Raza, now UnidosUS, a nonprofit civil rights organization, and on the difficulties of staying true to a mission amid the endless and often torturous search for funding. She captured a simple truth that others have echoed: "institutional resilience" requires "knowing what your North star is and knowing what your purpose is."[9] In other words, knowing what work you are called to do and why.

———

Resilience has become a buzzword of our time, used to combat everything from climate change to burnout. Surveying what it has come to mean on college campuses, Georgetown history professor Marcia Chatelain points out an irony: students who overcome poverty and racial discrimination and manage to rise are praised for their resilience as an inherent trait, while far more privileged students are increasingly taking courses in resilience, on the assumption that it is a set of skills that can be taught.[10] These courses focus on techniques to reduce stress and increase focus, the tools of "adulting," and the development of a growth mindset.[11] Yet if resilience *can* be taught, then the failure to rise in the face of extreme adversity cannot be a character flaw so much as a lack of opportunity.

Chatelain suggests that instead of thinking about resilience as either an individual trait or skillset, we instead use a growing social and economic focus on resilience as a way "to interrogate inequality and its consequences." Why not focus more on the reasons that some parents are less able to provide for their children than others? Or that some communities are less able to adapt to economic crises or the impact of climate change than others? The focus on what is missing shifts the responsibility for success away from individuals who find a way to thrive against the odds to the responsibility for changing those odds in the first place.[12]

This approach makes sense, particularly if we use the Marstons' concept of "transformative resilience," a version of which resurfaced in a quite unexpected place. In 2019, Walmart and McKinsey published a report titled *America at Work*. The researchers categorized every single county in the United States as one of eight different economic types (rural hubs, urban, resource- or recreation-based, distressed Americana, etc.) and assessed them in terms of how well prepared they are for the coming automation of many current jobs. Each county was measured in terms of different categories of "resiliency," defined as "the capacity to change."[13]

One of the constants across all eight categories, the researchers found, was that an effective response to approaching automation "will require community-level collaboration by multiple stakeholder groups."[14] That is jargon for increasing connections between people in different social groups and economic sectors. Political scientist Sean Safford would not be surprised by this conclusion. In his wonderfully titled book *Why the Garden Club Couldn't Save Youngstown*, he demonstrated convincingly that the most resilient communities, in terms of withstanding economic shocks, are those able to build on connections of many different kinds.[15]

The idea that the country would benefit from more connection is not exactly new. Harvard professor Robert Putnam has been writing for three decades, prophetically and accurately, about the decline of American social capital, which he defined back in 2001 as "connections among individuals—social networks and the norms of reciprocity and trustworthiness that arise from them."[16] The Baltimore-based organization Thread, founded in 2004, helps young people in poor and disconnected neighborhoods by "creating connection" among students, university and community volunteers, and collaborating organizations.[17] Thread's tagline is "the new social fabric": its goal is to connect students to jobs, internships, support services, and the whole range of opportunities that affluent communities take for granted. Just think how often you have done a favor for a friend by connecting someone in her life to someone in yours. Indeed, "having connections" is a synonym for having power and agency.

The Aspen Institute's Weave project seeks to take this strategy national, with a manifesto and playbook for "weavers" across the country.[18] Imagine what the threads of connection might be in your community. What kinds of connections could you make for a teenager looking for a summer job, a mother looking for childcare, a senior seeking companionship? What relationships could you nurture as they grow and flower?

—————

As a society, we could be bolder still by caring much more about care. Care is the strongest source of human connection, from our earliest days to our last breath. Western societies make the grievous mistake of thinking about care primarily as a service: feeding, bathing, dressing, toileting, medicating, accompanying, and otherwise tending to a set of largely physical needs. Good care, however—the care we want and need—is not a service but a *relationship*. The physical connection it typically requires supports the emotional connection that is essential to human well-being and development.

All parents or other caregivers for young children, for instance, know that bath time, mealtime, or even time on the changing table is but the scaffolding for talking, playing, soothing, or teaching. For an older person, good care consists of enabling the person to have what doctor and medical journalist Atul Gawande calls his or her "best day"—the best day possible under the circumstances of a particular illness or condition.[19] For any other person needing care, whether temporarily or permanently, the goal is to comfort and heal, but also to enable and empower.

Caregivers benefit as much from this connection as the cared for. I owe this insight to Milton Mayeroff, a philosopher and a father, who wrote a slim volume *On Caring* in 1971.[20] He described caring as "self-actualization" through the growth of others, a simultaneous extension of self and appreciation of the autonomy and ability of the other.[21] Understood this way, care is the glue bonding families together, the way in which family members invest in and nurture one another's well-being. I refer to families both as biologically related groups of people and groups who come together out of love and long-term commitment to one another. However constructed, they are the ultimate source of strength and resilience in a community.

Supporting care requires policies like paid family and medical leave, affordable and high-quality childcare and eldercare for working caregivers, and an entire revaluation of the social and financial worth of caregivers. Care given inside the home, largely by women, has traditionally been ignored in economic terms as a "labor of love"; care provided outside the home, still almost entirely by women and disproportionately by Black and brown women, is woefully underpaid.

The COVID-19 pandemic has put care on the front lines and the front pages: care workers of many different kinds, from nurses to teachers to home health aides, are essential workers; mothers suddenly deprived of help in caring for their children are leaving the workforce in large numbers. In short, the fragility of the American care infrastructure and the resulting vulnerability of our society and economy is on full display. We are a far less resilient nation as a result.

Running toward the criticism, whether in our own lives, our workplaces, or our national life, will put a premium on resilience. We must be able to take that criticism and use it as a springboard for transformation, understanding the necessity of connection to others and the value of collective purpose.

Having a new appreciation of the value and necessity of the relationships in my own life, personal and professional, gave me a new perspective on my own past. It was time to look backward in another way, to reassess a character trait I *did* think I possessed, and take another look at where it came from. I had always thought of myself as a risk taker.

CHAPTER 3

Rethink Risk

Renewal is risky business. It is impossible to grow, to learn, to bring something new into the world without taking risks. That's scary, but at least these are risks you choose to take, rather than the hidden risks of staying the same, clinging to what you know even as the world changes around you.

In the fall of 2017 I would lie awake and worry, images of disaster looming larger and larger, thoughts that might in the light of day give way to reason burrowing deeper and deeper into my brain. In particular, I would wonder what had possessed me to leave the security of academia for the far riskier life of a nonprofit leader. A tenured position as a university professor means a guaranteed salary for life. Nonprofit leaders, on the other hand—think everything from CARE or Amnesty International to your local charity—spend a huge portion of our time fundraising. Our ability to do the work we do, and often our own salaries, depend on the willingness of others to support our work.

Before continuing, let me make something clear. I am well aware that to *have* choices between different high-level jobs and career paths is a mark of privilege and status, both of which I have achieved not only through my own ambition and hard work but also by being given a huge boost on life's ladder at birth. I was born into a white, upper-middle-class family, a tremendous advantage in American and global society.

I know now just how much that foundation, cushion, safety net—however you want to think about it—made it far easier for me to take risks. Even so, I can only tell you my own story. Jumping a chasm—even metaphorically—can still feel plenty scary even when you recognize that other people are standing on the edge of far deeper and wider ravines.

Most important, through reading and reflection over the past couple of years, I have come to realize that although risk taking is to some extent a matter of personality and courage, it is also a straightforward calculation of costs and benefits.[1] If the costs of failure are high, then to make it worthwhile to take the risk, the estimated benefits—the scale of the imagined opportunity—must be correspondingly high. How high you are willing to try to climb depends in most cases on how far you think you can fall.

That insight, backed by scholarly research, has personal and national implications. As the economist Mariana Mazzucato argues, in the economy of the future, "de-risking" will be impossible; it must be replaced by "welcoming uncertainty."[2] Most Americans are experiencing far too much uncertainty already; to enable them to take the risks necessary for their personal and professional growth, policymakers at the local, state, and federal levels will have to provide, paradoxically, much more security.

Shortly after I became dean of Princeton's School of Public and International Affairs in 2002,[3] I was asked to give the commencement address at Greenwich Academy, an affluent private school where girls still graduate in white dresses carrying

flowers, much as I did at St. Anne's-Belfield School in Charlottesville in 1976. I crafted a talk that I have used as the basis of
many subsequent addresses, on the theme: "Take Risks, Take
Time, Take Care."

I will not take you through each segment; suffice it to say that
it works for a commencement crowd prepared to sit through
ten minutes of life advice. The point is precisely the one I made
above: risk taking is absolutely essential for personal and professional growth. My advice to my children and mentees is that
if your stomach doesn't hurt when you start a new job or head
for the first day of school or try something you have never done
before, then you are not far enough out of your comfort zone
to learn anything. You have to embrace the fear, or at least accept it, even when what you really want to do is go home and
curl up in bed.

Everyone from my family to my accountant to my New
America colleagues would describe me as highly risk acceptant.
I have changed jobs, and indeed careers, roughly every six to
eight years, zigzagging in ways I never planned or expected.
Quite the contrary: I entered college with my life completely
mapped out, planning to go to law school and then to a big New
York law firm with an international practice, where I expected
to make a career as an "in and outer" in the State Department.
I had researched foreign policy careers and knew that the top
State Department positions were traditionally filled by political
appointees who backed the right candidate or had the right
mentor and could spend periods when their party was in power
in government and then go back to their law firms (or other
private-sector jobs) when the political tides changed.

I *never* thought of becoming an academic. Indeed, the one
profession I would have absolutely rejected when I graduated
from college in 1980 was being a professor. I had no interest in

what I saw as a contemplative rather than an active life, writing books rather than making things happen in the world.

I did go to law school and I did work for one summer for a big New York law firm—one where many of the partners had followed exactly the in-and-out pattern to which I aspired. The firm welcomed me (and the fifty other mostly white and majority male summer associates they hired that summer); it was the go-go eighties, when firms competed with one another to wine and dine potential hires. The partners and permanent associates were interesting people who prided themselves on a strong culture of integrity. And when the summer was over, they gave me an offer to join the firm after graduation.

There was only one problem with my grand plan. I had never actually thought about the work that I would be doing day in and day out in that big New York law firm I planned to join. As it turned out, I was miserable. It was not the firm's fault; it was the nature of the practice. I was working on big corporate deals where I sometimes didn't even know who the client was or what was being traded; I felt completely fungible with all the other associates (we were defined entirely by our résumés); and as what would now be called a "smart creative,"[4] I was not well suited to the predictable hours and routines of office life.

I said no to the offer. That left me with two fancy postgraduate degrees but no plan. I enrolled in a Ph.D. program chiefly to be eligible for various predoctoral fellowships (to apply for funding, you actually have to be in a predoctoral program) and kept working for Abram Chayes, one of Harvard Law School's most brilliant professors, who became my mentor, role model, dear friend, and ultimately colleague. I loved that work, but I never imagined that it would actually lead to a career in academia itself. And certainly nothing in my law school career suggested that I had the makings of a law professor.

But the thing about saying no to things you don't want to do is that it then leaves you open to saying yes to things you discover you *do* want to do. I did not have the status, salary, or direction that would have come with being an associate at a big New York firm, but I had the time to accept an invitation to be part of a young leaders group from both East and West hosted by the Aspen Institute Berlin—the Berlin Wall was still up—which met four times over two years and introduced me to an entire group of young foreign policy experts who became friends and valuable contacts over the years.

I had the time to understand and accept that my six-year-old marriage was falling apart, and then to fall madly in love with Andy. And I had the time to imagine myself as a law professor, a career path that I came to understand would combine teaching and scholarship with enough direct connection to shaping and applying the law in real time to keep me happy.

In the grand scheme of things, falling off—or taking myself off—the well-established path to a legal career is hardly a huge risk. After all, I was married, and even though my first husband was also a student, we could cobble together enough income from various sources to live as a couple without children. If all else failed I could always go home to my parents in Virginia and regroup. I had college and graduate school degrees, so I was certainly well-credentialed. I also had the safety net of knowing that I could apply to law firms to be an associate and get back on a career track, even if it was a track I no longer wanted to be on.

Still, I *thought* I was taking both a financial and reputational risk, heading off on a path without knowing where it might lead, contravening the expectations of my peers and my parents. When I look back now, I realize two things: that I certainly don't look like the stereotypical American image of a risk taker, and that my safety net made all the difference. I was never in danger of losing my home, my health care, or my ability to make a living.

⸻

The face of risk taking in the United States is male, largely white, and flashy. Think Tom Cruise, who shot to stardom, appropriately enough, with the movie *Risky Business*, and has been the embodiment of male daredevilry over a lifetime of dramatic action films appropriately titled *Mission: Impossible*. The professional equivalent of hanging off cliffs and jumping crevasses is the Silicon Valley version of entrepreneurship: betting vast sums that you don't have on risky deals or maxing out your credit cards and borrowing from everyone you know to fund a start-up that countless people have told you is bound to fail (assuming, of course, that the people you know have funds to lend, which tells us immediately who cannot participate in this kind of risk taking).

In fact, women are just as inclined to take risks as men. Generations of studies on risk have supported a hypothesis that historian of science Cordelia Fine dubs "testosterone rex": "the idea that women are driven by biology and evolution to be cautious, and men to be daring." Natural selection supposedly favored men who were willing to take risks to hunt down food or fight other men for territory and thereby were rewarded with multiple mates, whereas women could have only one mate at a time.[5]

Fine carefully dissects this logic and the science behind it, citing multiple studies showing that risk taking is not a stable personality trait even among individuals, much less across genders. In other words, studies repeatedly show that people who are risk acceptant in some areas of their lives are risk averse in others, leading to "insurance-buying gamblers" and "skydiving wallflowers." If we cannot identify even individuals as uniformly arrayed along a spectrum from risk takers to risk avoiders, then how can we possibly classify entire groups that way?

What does come through the research time and again is that "the risk in a given situation is inherently subjective, varying from one individual to the next." Individuals engage in a subjective evaluation of the costs and benefits of a particular course of action, based on their own life experience and circumstances. When men and women have the *same* perception of the costs and benefits of a risk, they are equally likely to take it. But their perceptions often differ, just as the perceptions of men of color often differ from those of white men.

It is thus not surprising that many women are less willing to take at least some of the kinds of risks that men take; women who are caregivers must assess any potential dangers in terms of a possible threat not only to themselves but also to the others in their charge. The world is a much scarier place when you are responsible for those who need care, other humans who are by definition younger, older, weaker, sicker, or simply more vulnerable. The women in these situations are not actually less daring in some essential sense; they just rightly assess the risk to be much higher than a non-caregiving man would in the same situation.[6]

In situations where life experience does not shape perception to the same extent, men and women take the same amount of risk, but may do so differently. For instance, financial expert and neuroscientist John Coates has analyzed the behavior of male and female traders and finds that men like to take risks quickly, thrilling to the rapid-fire pace of the trading floor (think modern-day battlefield), whereas women prefer to take more time to analyze a security and then make the trade.[7]

In still other situations, women are actually *more* willing to take risks than men. One important category where this appears to be true is social risks—such as diverging from your friends or family in your opinions or tastes.[8] Let's think of that category as the risk of nonconformism—a critical attribute for an entrepreneur or for what organizational psychologist Adam Grant calls an "original," a person whose "hallmark is rejecting the default and exploring whether a better option exists."[9] A vibrant, innovative society wants more of exactly those people.

So, who is really taking risks in our society and how can we encourage more of it? Consider the cost-benefit analysis that a parent makes who is contemplating moving to another neighborhood to send a child to a better school, typically leaving behind family, friends, and an entire infrastructure of social support. The costs are evident, but are the benefits? Can such parents be sure that their children will get the attention and support they need to flourish? Can they fully envision the many doors that might open for their children as a result of both a better education and a whole new set of valuable contacts?

Similarly with the young person who is the first in their family to go to college, following all the advice about the lifelong value of a college degree. If I think back to how scared *I* was to go to college, a path everyone in my family had followed, with all the support in the world, and with classmates who overwhelmingly looked like me and came from similar backgrounds, I cannot imagine taking those steps for the first time, deeply uncertain of success and with plenty of voices whispering that I was crazy or a fool to try.

We need not look at risk taking case by case, however, comparing individuals and their families. Michelle Gelfand, a

sociologist at the University of Maryland, has conducted exten-
sive research on what she calls "tight" versus "loose" cultures,
rule-makers versus rule-breakers.[10] Tight cultures are rule-
bound and strict, marked by deep social solidarity but little
room for individual innovation. Think Japan. Loose cultures are
the opposite: rules are just the start of a negotiation, individuals
put themselves apart from or ahead of the group, innovation
flourishes. Think Italy.

Many factors shape a culture: history, geography, demography, economics, and politics, to name just a few. Still, Gelfand
finds that groups under threat—whether at the family, local, or
national level—tighten up. It's obvious when you think about
it. The military, for instance, is the tightest, most rule-bound
culture there is. No one wants pushback when everyone's lives
are at stake. Gelfand points to South Korea and India as examples of tight cultures, both of which face a perceived national
threat from neighboring countries.

Threats come in many forms other than neighboring armies.
Consider the many African American parents who brook no
argument over their children following the rules when it comes
to dealing with authority, in the form of a teacher, an employer,
or a cop—authority that is still overwhelmingly white. As Kiese
Laymon tells it, his mother, a political scientist in Jackson, Mis-
sissippi, insisted he be "excellent, disciplined, elegant, emotionally contained, clean, and perfect in the face of American white
supremacy."[11]

Now consider which parents encourage, or at least tolerate,
risk taking. Mark Zuckerberg dropped out of Harvard, not
community college, to found Facebook. Silicon Valley is full of
young, mostly white men from relatively well-off families who
went to prestigious schools, who could imagine reaching for the
stars in part because they would not fall very far if they failed.
Indeed, Silicon Valley has made a cult of failure as the path to

learning, urging entrepreneurs to "fail fast"[12] and move on to their next venture.

Failure *is* the path to learning. But what if you have no savings and no parents to bail you out? What if failure means not being able to make rent or put food on the table? Giving up your health care? Not just losing your job, but the ability to get another one? What if those threats, largely abstractions for upper-middle-class kids, are all too real?

Poor cultures are tight cultures. If we want people to break the rules, to innovate, to believe that they can shape their own lives, and to build and create something new, then we need to make them feel safer. It almost seems un-American to say so, but risk taking requires security.

As a matter of national policy, it is time to move beyond a social safety net, a New Deal idea created to catch people when they fall and forestall complete destitution. To enable Americans to meet the challenges of future job markets in an era in which up to 50 percent of current jobs may be eliminated due to technological change, we must create an entire social infrastructure designed to support creativity, innovation, and lifelong learning.

Imagine a children's play structure, with a sturdy foundation, ropes and ladders in different directions, tunnels that open up in surprising places, and slides and sawdust pits for rapid exits and soft landings. We design those structures to allow kids to explore and test their limits, to help them grow and learn. Americans can build a social infrastructure that will do the same for all our people, allowing them the space and security necessary to figure out how to make their own living.

Government support may not be able to equalize all opportunity, but it can replicate at least some of what good fortune and strong families provide. If government can invest in innovation, as it has so often before, launching technologies from the Internet to the iPhone, it can also invest in innovators.[13]

Examples of the ways in which greater security can spur greater risk taking are not hard to find. The flood of young people willing to try their hand at start-ups in Silicon Valley and across the country was spurred in part by the Obama administration's expansion of parental health insurance for children until age twenty-six.[14] Before that, young people leaving high school or college had to find jobs in the regular workforce as fast as possible—or stay in school—to ensure that they moved from their parents' health insurance to their employers'. In a similar vein, the nation's artists, in some ways our ultimate risk takers, spoke up in strong support of Obamacare.

Health insurance ensures that an illness or accident does not mean bankruptcy and years of debt that is nearly impossible to repay.[15] Health insurance cannot provide the means to launch a new enterprise, however, whether a small business or a start-up designed to scale. It is deeply telling that the vocabulary of venture capital begins with "the friends and family round": the initial funds that an entrepreneur can rustle up in $10,000 and $20,000 increments from parents, grandparents, aunts, uncles, siblings, college roommates, elementary school friends who have struck it rich, and anyone else to whom the entrepreneur can appeal. People who don't have family and friends of means are out of luck.

According to the Federal Reserve, 40 percent of Americans would not be able to cover a four-hundred-dollar emergency without borrowing money or selling something, including 12 percent who simply would not be able to cover it at all.[16] If we believe that talent is equally distributed but opportunity is not, just think how many talented entrepreneurs, innovators, and creators we are leaving behind. Moreover, at a time when the future of work in the United States and many other countries in the world will require many more individuals to be self-employed, putting together multiple streams of income from different activities, a social infrastructure must be designed to enable people to create their own jobs.

Creating pools of capital guaranteed either by government or by impact investors and designed to provide initial rounds of funding to women entrepreneurs and entrepreneurs of color, all of whom currently get only a tiny fraction of investment capital, would help. In the wake of the COVID-19 pandemic, such capital will be more essential than ever to support an entire new generation of small and medium-sized businesses across the country, to replace the restaurants and retailers that have been wiped out. These investments may require a different definition of entrepreneurship and a different perspective on the kinds of returns that investors are looking for.

Many Americans think of a social infrastructure in terms of a European "nanny state," taking the risk out of life and hence undermining the self-reliance that so many Americans pride themselves on. It is certainly possible to go too far. Yet making affordable, high-quality, and genuinely universal public health care and education available to all Americans would simply create the social and economic conditions under which risk taking is a reasonable enterprise.

Other measures, such as creating portable benefits that would allow all workers to provide for periods when they will not be working in one account that they, their employers, and the government can add to over a lifetime, would again encourage risk taking—striking out for something new—by allowing people to leave their current jobs and look for new ones in different parts of the country.[17] The infrastructure of care discussed in the last chapter is equally essential, to give caregivers enough security to assess the costs and benefits of risks differently.

If we put these programs together, think of all the energy and innovation we could unlock, just as the building of a road or a bridge or a port allows people to move, trade, connect, and create. As of this writing, President Biden has introduced a number of bills designed to rebuild the nation's physical infrastructure and renew the very concept of infrastructure to include an entire set of vital care facilities. Such infrastructure will both create good care jobs and enable men and women with caregiving responsibilities to go to work if they want or need to.

Suppose, however, we brought a whole set of education, health, housing, labor, and care policies together to create the foundation for a new generation of entrepreneurs, men and women who would assess that the benefits of the risks necessary to bring something new into the world or to follow an uncharted path outweigh the costs. Call it the American Innovation Act, patterned on the sweeping provisions of the GI Bill of 1944, which provided education, housing, and unemployment insurance largely for returning white veterans. The GI Bill laid the foundation for the prosperity of a rapidly expanding white middle class in the 1950s and 1960s. The American Innovation Act would lay the foundation for a prosperous and sustainable new American economy, this time for all Americans.

Telescoping back to the personal level, I often think about how women can become more risk acceptant by supporting one another to be our truer selves. Let's be braver about saying what we really think in many situations, but often do not dare to voice.

I'll give you an example. I believe, as do many women—and probably a fair number of men—that spending our tax dollars on early education, shaping young brains in their first years of life so that they can learn and grow to their full potential for the rest of their lives, is just as important as spending money on national defense. Indeed, I believe that investing in the intelligence and capacity of our people should be the cornerstone of our national security.

The old me would never have dared to say that in a national security forum. The men and probably some women would have laughed me out of the room. Yet why shouldn't we invest as much in our children as our national defense? The long-term survival and prosperity of our people—indeed of the world's people and the world itself—depends just as much on teaching as killing. If we have the political will, we have enough resources for both.

Conversely, I recall that when I was working under Hillary Clinton at the State Department, she pioneered an initiative for clean cookstoves in communities across Africa and Asia, cookstoves that would simultaneously improve the health of families, reduce carbon emissions, and increase the security of the women and girls who are often attacked as they forage far and wide for wood. From the perspective of the women and a few men working on this initiative, it was a foreign policy trifecta. But to many of our male colleagues, men who thought *real* foreign policy is about going toe-to-toe with other governments to intimidate them or negotiate various kinds of deals, it was a diversion at best, and was often laughed at behind our backs.

The conversations in the State Department when only women were in the room varied sharply from the conversations when men and women were both present. But few of us—other than Secretary Clinton herself or her indomitable and fearless chief of staff, Cheryl Mills—dared to challenge the men directly. We should have.

We women can also be more willing to risk being ourselves, cracks and all, to fight against the relentless culture of digitally enhanced perfection. The twentieth-century literary critic Lionel Trilling delivered a famous set of lectures in 1969–70 that were published under the title *Sincerity and Authenticity*.[18] He pointed out that in museums, the hallmarks of authenticity are often more likely to be imperfection than perfection—the cracks, discoloration, and wear of age. In human relations, authenticity often flows from spontaneity—an immediate, unfiltered reaction that reveals imperfection.

Professor Brené Brown has built an entire practice on teaching us to live and lead by turning vulnerability into value, but it's harder than it sounds.[19] Hard for men, due to the constraints of traditional ideas and images of stoic masculinity. Hard for white women; harder still for women of color. National poet laureate Natasha Trethewey recalls that although her Northern white father "believed in the idea of living dangerously, the necessity of taking risks," her Southern Black mother "had witnessed the necessity of dissembling, the art of making of one's face an inscrutable mask before whites who expected of blacks a servile deference."[20]

Trethewey ultimately finds the courage to take after her father, telling the deeply personal and wrenching story of her mother's murder by her stepfather after decades of locking away her memories. She takes enormous risks, but her readers benefit. The United States as a whole will have to take similar risks of self-exploration and revelation; I hope women will insist on and lead in this more personal kind of emotional risk taking. We are, after all, more likely to take the risks of breaking the established social mold.

I have taken plenty of risks in my life, even if I now understand that I never really had that far to fall. I will now think differently, however, about the conditions under which I can encourage others to take risks. Back in 2017, I still had a risky road ahead, with plenty of opportunities to try and fail. To begin with, I wanted to find a new and better way to lead.

CHAPTER 4

Lead from the Center and the Edge

In November 2017, the New America board met and affirmed that I should keep my job, at least for the time being. They also decided that I needed a leadership coach, a view I embraced. I was still badly shaken and welcomed all the help I could get. I found the wonderful Penny Handscomb and worked with her for the next two years.

The irony is that I often write and lecture on leadership. We all know the cliché about "those who can't do, teach," but that's not the case here. I have led in various capacities for more than two decades, largely successfully. What is true, however, is that I had never sat down and figured out exactly how to practice what I preach.

When I give talks on leadership, I typically begin by introducing my audience to my favorite definition of leadership, developed by Nannerl Keohane in her book *Thinking about Leadership*. As Nan puts it, leaders "determine or clarify goals for a group of individuals and bring together the energies of members of that group to accomplish those goals."[1] It is a definition that does not depend on title, position, or authority—other than the authority conferred, temporarily or enduringly, by the members of the group. If you think about your various roles through this lens, you are likely to see that you are a leader in some places—your family, group of friends, a community organization—even if you are not in your workplace or other more formal settings.

Nan's definition of leadership is also much more horizontal than vertical. To explain what I mean by "horizontal," I have to take you on a brief detour. In 1982, when I was a first-year law student, social psychologist Carol Gilligan published a book titled *In a Different Voice: Psychological Theory and Women's Development*.[2] Harvard University Press, which published the book, describes it as "the little book that started a revolution";[3] it certainly did for me. Gilligan identified differences in the moral development of adolescent boys and girls, arguing that girls reasoned more in terms of an "ethic of care" and boys in an "ethic of justice." That observation elicited furious charges of gender stereotyping, debates that continue to this day.

The part of the book that rocked my world, however, was Gilligan's account of how the boys and girls she studied thought about relationships, contrasting a vertical hierarchy of dominance with a horizontal web of connection. If you think about relationships in terms of a hierarchy—a ladder, a pecking order—then you want to be at the top. But if you think about them in terms of a web, then you want to be at the center. The problem is that the top of the ladder becomes the edge of the web and the center of the web becomes the middle of the ladder; thus, "each image marks as danger the place which the other defines as safe."[4]

That insight was revelatory. I knew that I was much more interested in being at the center of things than being at the top, a trait that I thought of and faulted as a lack of ambition, given that ambition in a man's world meant getting to the top of whatever ladder you were on. But now I came to see that I actually just had a different way of seeing the world, and that power and leadership could actually be about connection as much as control. Over time, I have realized that is a perspective open to all humans, regardless of gender.

It's fair to say that Gilligan's insight has shaped my entire career: I've spent thirty years studying and writing about networks versus hierarchies as instruments of governance and problem solving. I've written an entire book chapter on leading horizontally, from the center of a web rather than from the top of the ladder, through tools of mobilization rather than command and control. Tools like clarifying interests, curating a specific set of connections, making and tending those connections, cultivating relationships designed to empower others, and catalyzing action.[5] Indeed, I have argued that the United States should think about global leadership this way, "from the center" rather than "from the top."[6]

I was lecturing on horizontal leadership, but practicing vertical leadership. New America is a hierarchy, in the sense that it has an org chart that shows power relationships from the top to the bottom. I was leading from the top, but trying at the same time to flatten that org chart and create more horizontal spaces where everyone could contribute and relate to one another differently. Yet in working with Penny, and then with my colleagues, I came to see a whole new dimension of what being "at the center" can mean, how if someone is at the center of a web, then someone else is always at the margin. I began to understand, and to try to practice, a way of leadership that still recognizes the necessity of exercising power over others, but also flattens those relationships and connects the center to the margin as much as possible.

———

I expected Penny to start our coaching sessions by conducting a thorough "360-degree review," an exercise in which people who work for you, with you, and above you review your performance—either through anonymous questionnaires or, ideally, mediated by a coach or external interviewer. These reviews have been a management "best practice" for a while now. Among other things, they help supervisors figure out when people who report to them are "kissing up and kicking down," a posture and practice that still surprises and saddens me even after years of being a boss.

When it's your turn to be the subject of such a review, empowering others to say what they really think about you based on what they actually see you do and hear you say can be a form of radical honesty. Think of it as looking into a mirror that is much harder to manipulate to show only your best side. Psychologist Jonathan Haidt describes us all as having an "in-house press secretary," the rational rider on the emotional elephant whose job it is to justify every action or decision the elephant makes, from the trivial to the consequential.[7] A good 360-degree review should be the ideal corrective.

Over time, trying to see yourself through others' eyes should become a reflex, a habitual check on what you are about to say or do. You must learn to be yourself and stand outside yourself at the same time. On the other hand, the people who work all around you—below, beside, and above—all have their own motives and biases that shape how they evaluate you. That's precisely why the best 360-degree reviews are conducted by coaches (the corporate term for therapists) who are empowered to interview your coworkers and filter out what appear to be biased results before sharing the reviews with you.

Penny, however, started from the inside out. She certainly talked to some of the people who worked with me, but her focus was much more on how I thought about myself and, above all, what I wanted to do more of. She was deeply affirming, even as she pushed and prodded at my feelings—that steady drumbeat of "shoulds." She gave me exercises—circles to draw, charts to make—all designed to get at what economists would call "revealed preferences": an academic term for what we really want rather than what we say or think we want.

As Penny and I worked together, I came to realize that I am happiest and most effective when I am connecting people; creating things, either by bringing new ideas into the world or building new programs or institutions; or by catalyzing action—being the spark that leads other people to create new things or to improve old ones. Even though I periodically imagine other paths, such as running for office or running really big institutions, the choices I have consistently made over my life tell a different story.

Penny helped me see that once you know what you are best at doing, a set of things that has a remarkable overlap with what you most like doing, you can build a team that complements those strengths and compensates for the inevitable accompanying weaknesses, and stop feeling guilty or inadequate for not being able to do everything. Equally important, if you relax enough, you can learn continually from the members of your team, and ultimately your whole organization, who encounter the world quite differently from the way you do. Leadership, like John Gardner's conception of renewal, can be a continuous process of learning and exploration.

Day by day, my best teachers were two women who became close colleagues and friends at New America. I have talked about both Tyra Mariani and Cecilia Muñoz already; let me introduce them more fully here.

Tyra grew up in New Orleans as the daughter of working-class African American parents; her father was a railroad switchman and her mother a customer service supervisor for an insurance company. Tyra went to Catholic school, which she credits with giving her the education and discipline that provided a springboard first to Howard University, one of the nation's finest historically Black universities, and then to Stanford Business School. Her early career was in education and education policy: she served as the budget director for the Chicago Public Schools and later as deputy chief of staff in the Department of Education in the Obama administration.

Tyra is an experienced coach herself and has spent enormous amounts of time figuring out her own strengths and weaknesses through various leadership trainings. As in all great working, educational, and personal relationships, she taught me as much as I taught her, even though she is nearly twenty years younger.

Cecilia is the daughter of Bolivian immigrants to Michigan. She spent decades fighting for the civil rights and equal treatment of all immigrants before joining the Obama administration, where she ended up as head of the Domestic Policy Council. A vice president and now senior adviser at New America since 2016, Cecilia is a deeply valued colleague and an author, mentor, role model, and inspiration to countless young women.

Tyra, Cecilia, and I have much in common: the foundation of a great education that has enabled all of us to enjoy upper-middle-class lifestyles, the pride and experience of working in the Obama administration, and the commitment to what Cecilia would call "trying to do good work in the world." Our common experiences as women in a man's world give us plenty to bond over. Still, I became aware of the ways in which our different backgrounds shaped our attitudes and expectations differently. I came to see the unalterable fact of both of their lives: we are all women, but Tyra's identity as a Black woman and Cecilia's identity as a Latina determine how people see and react to them in ways that my white identity never will.

The three of us built a relationship partly through the pleasure of spending time together and partly through the experience of shared leadership responsibility, which we exercised together with two other valued colleagues, Peter Bergen and Kevin Carey. I never lost sight of my role as the ultimate decider if things got sticky, but step one in leading more horizontally was more collective leadership. Making a practice of consultation and reflection was like a constant 360-degree review, a process of continually asking how the things you say and do land with others. To be successful, however, it is essential to work with people different enough from you to see the world differently but whom you trust to be honest about what they see.

To take one of many examples, I would periodically respond to some horrific outside event by writing a note to staff. I remember doing so on the occasion of the shooting at Pulse, a gay nightclub in Orlando, Florida, which killed forty-nine and wounded more than fifty people in June 2016. I wrote about the horror of the shooting and of the senseless hatred and anti-LGBTQ bias that motivated it. I recognized how that might be weighing on many staff members and urged people to recognize and address that burden as they needed to.

Nothing wrong with that. But Tyra raised a critical point that I had never thought of, though I certainly should have. If I was going to write notes about some external events but not others—say, about a mass shooting against the LGBTQ community but not about a single police shooting of a Black man or woman, an event that I now understand is a single event piled on top of so many others—then staff members would draw their own conclusions about what was important to me and, through me, to New America as a whole. On the other hand, where to draw the line? Given the regular horrors of many different kinds reported in U.S. news, I could find myself writing daily. I still do not have a hard and fast rule here, but I am now much more reflective about when I write and what I say.

Both Tyra and Cecilia could also, and often did, point out to me and other New America leaders how the expectations of many of our upper-middle-class staff members—with regard to salary, benefits, or time off—seem deeply entitled to other staff members who come from less privileged backgrounds. Given that wealth and privilege track racial divides in the United States, it is often staff members of color who see white staff members as having so much and yet wanting more. Tyra, in particular, has also helped me see the ways in which manager discretion over hiring and salaries, which I tend to favor out of a desire not to bureaucratize everything, can be an invitation to inequity in a world of unconscious bias.

To some readers, these insights may seem obvious. They often now do to me. But they were not obvious four years ago, and it took people I trusted and respected, as colleagues but also as friends, to help me challenge views and certainties built up over many years of leadership. The road to better leadership requires understanding that good intentions are never enough.

⸻

Tyra and Cecilia were also conduits for staff members of color at New America who might otherwise have felt they had no one to talk to who would truly understand how they felt about specific incidents, words, or behaviors that made them feel

excluded or demeaned. All the affinity groups and formal griev-
ance processes in the world won't make a difference unless
some people in the organization can and will speak truth to
power. The younger you are or the lower down in the org chart
you are, the harder that is.

I had always thought that leading from the center of a web
was better than leading from the top of a hierarchy because relationships in a web were more equal. I also prefer non-
controlling forms of power, and would frequently cite Mary
Parker Follett, known as "the mother of modern management,"
for her concept of "power with" others rather than "power over"
them.[8] I love the idea and the practice of leading in a way that
empowers others to take initiative and build their own
relationships.

As I started to hear more from voices who had felt excluded,
however, I started to think about the relationship between the
center and the margin. It is impossible to locate the center of
something without also identifying the margin, whether it is the
circumference of a circle or the least connected nodes of a network or web. We call oppressed, dispossessed, stigmatized people
"marginalized" because they have been pushed to the edges of the
web of human connections that constitutes a society.

Leading from the center without paying constant attention
to the margin can substitute the horizontal power of exclusion
for the vertical power of domination. I often tell people that
power in Washington flows from the Oval Office in the White
House outward in a series of ever wider circles of who gets to
be "in the meeting" and who gets left out. Yet I had never focused on what those circles of inclusion might look like from
the perspective of those I lead.

I now believe that effective leadership from the center must
actually be leadership from the center *and* the edge.[9] It is

impossible to get anything done if everyone is included and consulted all the time; in my experience, leadership by consensus is often disastrous, shifting power to the most stubborn or the most passionate or sometimes the most obnoxious person in the room. Asking what others think, however, particularly those who have the least opportunity to make their voices heard in a group or organization, and really listening to the answers, without flinching or arguing, will benefit everyone involved. Engaging one another in ways that disrupt the usual hierarchy, such as by asking younger members of the staff to present a program's work, or by engaging in community activities in which titles are irrelevant, are other ways. Perhaps most important, administrative staff, from janitors to executive assistants, should be eligible to apply and be considered for any job in the organization that they have the skills for, regardless of their formal credentials.

Call it high school in reverse. Think back to your high school days, and you can immediately remember who was part of the "in crowd" and who was not, the finely calibrated degrees of inclusion and exclusion. Suppose now the test of success or popularity or worth is who can expand the club.

Almost all of us are leaders at some point in some parts of our lives, domains where we step into the role of determining or clarifying the goals of a group and mobilizing the energies of group members to achieve them. Each of us, thus, has some chance to lead from the center, in ways that empower others and are as equal as possible, and from the margin, in ways that are not just inclusive but disruptive. And all of us, as Americans or citizens of any other country, have a chance to change how we see and engage one another from the center to the margin.

All of us can think of ourselves as the hubs of our own circles: of family, friends, coworkers, and community members. How many people in your circle are of another race, ethnicity, class background, religion, or political affiliation? Probably not many.

You can change that. You can widen those circles, certainly by hiring people who are very different from yourself but also by thinking about the social activities you engage in, from sports teams to book clubs to choirs, and deliberately inviting different people to join. You can also try to turn acquaintance-ship into friendship by inviting someone you know only slightly from work or as a fellow school parent for coffee or a drink. The country needs this kind of outreach from people in different political parties as well, not as some kind of grand political reconciliation, but rather as an effort to see one another as human beings rather than as partisans.

In the process, we must learn to see ourselves in one another's eyes and not run from the reflection. I have talked about radical honesty in looking back to face our past; it is now time to learn how to engage one other in the present. We do not have to agree. We don't even have to change one another's minds, although it would be great if we could, at least a little. We just have to look and listen, reserving judgment, until we can find some common interest or identity around which we can identify as "we."

Given how politically segregated many parts of the country are, together with enduring racial and ethnic segregation, some of this work may need to be done virtually rather than physically. It is also always possible to turn to books, movies, TV series, even YouTube channels. In the wake of George Floyd's murder, places like Amazon and Netflix, as well as independent bookstores, offered lists of books and essays to read and videos to watch that are often the equivalent, for an affluent white person like me, of traveling to another world. It's possible to expand the number of people you follow on social media and make sure you deliberately try to follow people very different from yourself.[10] The ways in which social media companies use algorithms to surround you with the views only of people you agree with and then push you toward membership in an ever more extreme club is actually "antisocial media."[11] Push back as hard as you can.

Be prepared to read or watch without pushing back, doing your best to put your own preconceptions or reactions aside. To take just one example, back in the 1970s, the members of the Combahee River Collective identified "racism in the white women's movement" as an issue of major concern. "As Black feminists," they wrote, "we are made constantly and painfully aware of how little effort white women have made to understand and combat their racism, which requires among other things that they have a more than superficial comprehension of race, color, and Black history and culture."[12]

Surely, I think, that was then. Yet forty years later, a majority of white women voted for a presidential candidate who had bragged about grabbing women by the genitals and openly fanned the flame of racial division by exploiting the worst stereotypes of Black Americans as dangerous, lazy, or radical. For Rutgers professor Brittney Cooper, "white women's voting practices tell us that they vote with the party that supports their racial issues, even though this means voting with a party that hates women as a matter of public policy."[13]

Many women voters who chose Donald Trump would likely say, "I'm neither sexist nor racist, but I put economic issues first and Trump would have been better for the economy." Many liberal women voters like me would point to the tens of millions of white women who voted for Biden and say, "not *all* white women are like that." Both responses may well be true. Yet how would *I* feel if a majority of women of color in this society (a completely constructed category that is a far cry from a voting bloc) voted for a candidate who openly attacked white people? Knowing that many women of color felt differently or that other issues may have been in play would do little to diminish my sense of alienation, rejection, and fear.

In a more personal vein, sociologist and public intellectual Tressie McMillan Cottom writes about white standards of beauty (blonde, thin) and the ways Black girls and women are thereby taught to hate their bodies. As she reflects back on how white teachers responded to her large-breasted developing body in grade school, she formulates a warning that encapsulates so much of the way Black women encounter the world. "If I knew to be cautious of men," she writes, "I did not learn early enough to be cautious of white women."[14]

I read this work and learn from it. It is hard not to be defensive; I'm human. I remind myself, however, of the culture of strenuous debate I was taught as a young academic at the University of Chicago Law School, where a scholar would present her or his work and the first question would often start with, "I think you're completely wrong." I remind myself also of the nasty stereotype of "angry Black women," singling out Black women who dare to say what they think as people to fear and shun. As the members of the Combahee River Collective also observed, and as is still true, Black women in the United States and other majority-white countries are on the bottom of every hierarchy and at the margin of every web. They have every reason to be furious, to express what Brittney Cooper calls "eloquent rage." Not that they need my or any one else's permission.

Hearing that rage and accepting it is not the same as taking action against the conditions that produce it. But it is a first and necessary step, one that all of us can take. Remember feeling excluded, being on the margin of some group you wanted to be at the center of, even if you couldn't allow yourself to admit it. Imagine something better and take even a small step to make it happen.

As I read the writings of women who seem to attack me personally but are really attacking a category of women to which I belong, an entire structure of class and race that I am part of, I also believe that if I were to meet these authors, we would find some common ground based on common experiences. Perhaps the shared experience of loving and worrying about a child (that's true with fathers, too, but many fathers are still not as engaged in their children's lives as mothers are). Perhaps the experience of feeling like a sex object, or of being ignored or invisible in mostly male environments. Perhaps, with older women, the experience of going through menopause and watching our bodies change. Finding that common ground would not negate or deny our differences, but it might connect us enough to allow us to listen, learn, and change.

In all these conversations, we can be civil, respectful, engaged and engaging, willing to listen in the same way that we expect to be listened to. As women, we can continually challenge assumptions and convictions that we recognize are the product of a world designed by men for men, predominantly white men in the United States and Europe but also by men of every race and color around the world. We can find enough connections, in some parts of our lives, to imagine ourselves as part of what political scientists John Ahlquist and Margaret Levi call "a community of fate," a community in which members see an injury to one as an injury to all.[15]

As different groups of women, however, we must in turn expect to be challenged: white women by women of color, straight women by women of different sexual orientations, cisgender women by transgender or gender fluid women, and all women by men who reject masculine gender stereotypes. Women on the left should also expect to be challenged by women on the right, and vice versa. Our disagreements, however, should not mean we cannot see and hear one another as humans.

I am bolstered in this hope by my experience of learning to lead in a new way next to Tyra and Cecilia, forging relationships of enough trust and support to be able to hear hard things and see through different eyes. I think about how those changes at the personal level opened new paths to thinking about the work that is critically important to do for my organization and my nation. I think about the next step: learning to let go, at least a little, of the power and privilege so many of us hoard.

CHAPTER 5

Share Power

By September 2018, a year after the crisis, I was in a very different place. On my birthday that month, Tyra and I went to dinner and I offered her a promotion from executive vice president to president and chief operating officer. I had been president and CEO since 2013 and would now remain CEO, formally at the top of the org chart with Tyra just under me. In reality, however, she and I led New America as partners for the next two years, each with a primary area of responsibility but talking and consulting constantly.

Deciding to share power was one of the best decisions I ever made, an arrangement that I have continued with Tyra's successor. At first, however, it felt odd and a little scary. I remember sitting along the side of the table in the first leadership team meeting that Tyra chaired, wondering if I had sidelined myself in more ways than one. I soon recovered my balance, however, and it was clear to me that when it came to keeping us on time, on task, and within budget, Tyra had the skills we needed, in addition to her policy experience, just as we needed my vision, energy, connections, and creativity.

As we worked together in the coming years, I discovered other kinds of power that could be shared, less visibly but perhaps more deeply. The power to evaluate performance, for instance, which all too often flows only from the top down. The power to gather information and ideas before making a decision, which is often highly structured, with specific people designated as advisers or members of advisory councils of various kinds. And the power to persuade others, which typically can come from formal authority—in which case it is not clear whether the people under you actually agree with or merely acquiesce to what you are saying—or from the ability to set the agenda in such a way that your favored option is the only one that makes sense.

Power shared is not the same as power delegated. It is shared within the give and take of a human relationship, seesawing back and forth. It can be shared temporarily, informally, or only for very specific purposes. In most cases, the person doing the sharing gets back more than she expected or asked for.

As a nonprofit, mission-driven organization, New America has a social compact. Its seven articles are posted on the wall in the communal dining area. Article 6 is titled: "We can take it." The text reads: "We are committed to a growth mindset, which means that feedback is essential, at all levels and in all directions." Further on, we talk explicitly about "fearless feedback," about how growth requires feedback that points to the need for improvement—otherwise known as criticism. And indeed, we claim that "we don't hold back," that we encourage direct dialogue and frank conversations among colleagues.

I have told my story of running toward the criticism, of asking for honest feedback and getting it in the immediate wake of the crisis. Going forward, however, I had to figure out how to make those feedback loops more or less continual. One way was to encourage active and continual "managing up." With Tyra and Cecilia, it was really more about managing sideways, but the point is to create enough trust and receptivity to get people to tell you when they disagree with you, when you are pushing too hard, or when you need to let them do their jobs and stop micromanaging.

New America has held periodic sessions for staff members on "how to manage up," sessions that I always start by telling an early story of Tyra's and my time working together. Shortly after she came on as executive vice president, I emailed her to ask about something on a weekend. New America has strong norms about expecting people to work hard when they are on but also giving them real time off, and Tyra thought I should be modeling them. She waited a bit, and then wrote a very nice email back explaining that she often did not check her email on weekends but of course I could reach her by text for anything urgent. Message received! And rightly so.

That is a small example; I have plenty of others, including feedback from staff members that filtered up to me through members of the leadership team that led me to refocus entire programs. The point is that by talking openly about managing up as well as down, we are signaling that the power to evaluate and give feedback flows in both directions. It is shared, at least to some extent, between supervisors and supervisees.

Another management challenge is people who seem oblivious to patterns of reactions in the people they work with, unaware that perhaps they are the cause. John Gardner cites the example of the "hostile person who keeps asking: 'Why are people so hard to get along with?'"[1]

What question do you find yourself continually asking, from one relationship to another, one job to another? I can think of many for myself, but as a leader, one connected cluster of questions would be: "Why are people so resistant to change? Why can't they see and agree with where I want to take them? Why don't they trust me more?"

I know the answers now. Change, in an organization or a country, takes trust, and trust takes *time*. Time to hang out and talk to people or, more important, listen to them. Time to engage in ways that are noninstrumental, that are not meetings with an agenda and a goal. I was once a smoker; I remember many conversations had and friendships formed over cigarette breaks. I'm unquestionably healthier now, and have been for thirty years, but like many of my peers, I tend to value my time mostly in terms of what I can "get done."

Early on in my deanship, I recall one of my staff members urging me to make time just to walk the halls, check in with faculty members, go to events where others were presenting even when I wasn't asked to introduce or moderate. Parents who are primary caregivers for children will recognize this problem: the need to be ruthlessly efficient during the day. I did have young children at home when I was dean, but I was also chronically overcommitted. My days were always jammed with meetings and travel; I focused more on the world outside than the people inside.

At New America it was even harder, because I was in Washington only a couple of days a week at most. And to be as honest as we all need to be to make room for renewal, I had many other activities on my plate—some of which were directly related to New America but some of which were not. With this constant time crunch, unproductive time—in the sense of time not specifically committed to a task or goal—seemed pointless.

Gradually, however, I have come to see that "hanging out," sitting at the common lunch table, leaving open time on my schedule for "office hours," for which anyone can sign up to just come talk or ask questions, or taking time just to check in with people is not only essential for building real relationships, but can be another way of sharing power. Asking staff members what they think about something on your mind—a real decision that you are pondering, assuming you are not divulging confidential information—and taking their answers seriously broadens the circle of those who are consulted for their advice.

Better still is keeping a mind open enough to actually be persuaded. I no longer remember where I read that the best way to persuade someone else of something is to be willing to be persuaded yourself. It has certainly worked in parenting; allowing a child to change your mind through reasoned argument makes it much easier to change their mind in return. In trying to lead as horizontally as possible, I sometimes think that the measure of success in horizontal leadership is how often I change my mind—at least before a decision is taken. Bringing that attitude to conversations with employees at every level is a way of genuinely sharing the power of decision, at least for the length of a conversation.

A final dimension of shared power is greater accountability. Ensuring that others are not afraid to challenge you is a way of holding yourself to what you say you believe in. As lawyers well know, often the very process of describing a proposed action or decision to a group of people whom you respect and regard as your peers will expose the flaws in your logic or the gap between what you are proposing and your professed principles.

That is precisely why judges are required to give reasons for their decisions, so that members of the public can judge in their turn whether those reasons hold up in light of the body of principles and commitments enshrined in the law.[2]

I often find that when I have thought up a new idea, which always seems absolutely brilliant to me in the first flush of enthusiasm, my desire to proceed with it quickly and unilaterally is often a subconscious sign that I know if I expose it to scrutiny there may be some good reason not to go ahead. It is common knowledge today, even if often not practiced, that having a diverse team avoids groupthink and spurs innovation, such that consultation will result in better ideas. All true. In my case, however, forcing myself to consult with my team, even when I really don't want to, is a way of slowing myself down and, above all, holding myself accountable.

It is not always efficient. Indeed, Tyra would say that I sometimes slow things down and complicate matters because I am too worried about just making the decision myself and moving forward. She's right; the balance can be hard to strike. Efficiency, however—more, more, more with less, less, less—has been the mantra of the American corporate sector for several decades now, with questionable results for the country as a whole.

Consider the Silicon Valley nostrum "move fast and break things."[3] It has become a watchword for disruption and innovation, but I have learned the hard way that it can also break you. The extra time it takes to run an idea by others or ensure that the right people are in the loop is actually time spent weaving a web of inclusion and accountability.

Imagine if more leaders of all kinds of organizations, including politicians, spent more time "walking the halls"—of Congress, City Hall, warehouses and factory floors, civic organizations, even virtual spaces created truly to engage one another rather than to execute a specific task. Imagine if the point were to float ideas and hear responses, as inclusively and nondefensively as possible. Consultation—*real* consultation, with an open mind and a willingness to be persuaded—is itself a form of sharing power, one that can be practiced from the CEO suite to the White House to the United Nations.

None of these practices mean that a hierarchy does not exist at New America, or at any organization or company that engages in practices similar to those I am describing. Some people are paid more than others and wield more authority over hiring, firing, and organizational direction and decisions than others. Some people have more freedom to determine how they will organize their workday and prioritize their time than others. Power relationships are still much more vertical than horizontal.

Still, I and my fellow leaders continually try to create channels for ideas and information to circulate in any direction and to create an environment in which people feel empowered to question and challenge proposed courses of action. My ideal would be an environment in which many people feel that they can lead on a specific project or initiative, where they can bring a group together, clarify goals, and mobilize energies. To build an organization flexible enough to be vertical for some purposes, as it must be, but horizontal for others, encouraging people to interact as equals and allowing information, feedback, and self-correction to flow in all directions.

That is possible. General Stanley McChrystal has written about how to take the members of a group and unite them for the purposes of developing a "shared consciousness"—that is, have all the same information and the same understanding of that information—and then split them up into smaller groups for "empowered execution": independent action in service of the common mission.[4] What I like about this way of leading is that different configurations of the same group can serve different purposes and have different power relationships, depending on specific form and function. When the group comes together for the purposes of sharing information, anyone can speak and be listened to; in the field with small groups, with lives on the line, one person has to be the commander.

If light can be both a wave and particle and a photon can exist in two different polarization states at the same time, whatever they may be, then surely a team, even a whole organization, can be flat for some purposes and vertical for others. Our world is moving too fast to lock everyone into only one relationship with one another.

Can leaders share power beyond their own organizations, at the local, state, and national level? Many observers of the United States would point out that the framers' system of separation of powers among the legislature, executive, and judiciary is actually a system of separated but often shared powers, with so many checks and balances that nothing can get done. Parliamentary systems, for instance, do not allow for a head of government of one party trying to pass laws through a legislature held by another party. In presidential systems that is possible, but for the past fifteen years in the United States, the two parties have been so unalterably opposed to each other that sharing really means blocking.

A new kind of shared power is emerging in the United States, however, borrowed from protest movements in other countries.

It is a kind of distributed power growing from the ground up, one that succeeds in being national and local at the same time. Consider the national and global Black Lives Matter movement, a coalition of many different organizations and networks, which explicitly embraces "horizontal leadership" and a nonhierarchical structure.[5]

The ideal of "leaderless revolutions" first emerged with the color revolutions in Georgia, Ukraine, and Moldova in the 2000s and then the Arab Spring beginning in 2011, but those revolutions were never leaderless so much as mobilized by multiple leaders working together in deeply flexible structures, often through social media.[6] Similarly, when Black Lives Matter coalesced as a movement in the United States, the cofounders avoided the kind of formal leadership roles and titles that characterized the civil rights movement of the 1960s. They instead created a chapter structure that "lets anyone step up and take responsibility for leadership tasks. It also enables multiple members to lead at the same time."

A frequent critique of these loose networked structures is that they work to mobilize protests and even revolutions, but make it very hard to actually govern or get things done. Yet to address the big, complex, deeply interconnected problems we face globally and nationally, we don't have clear answers that can simply be implemented. Problems like "climate change, destruction of ecosystems, the growing scarcity of water, youth unemployment, and embedded poverty and inequity," require "systems change," a fancy way of saying that we have to figure out how to change many interacting things all at once.[7] The problem of water scarcity, for instance, might be solved by cheap and rapid desalination, turning saltwater into freshwater. Yet how to get that water to the places that need it? How to change agricultural practices so that farmers use less water?

How to provide financing to make all of this possible? And on and on. There are simply too many moving parts to be solved by any one individual or group of people, no matter how smart they are.

Systems change requires systems leadership, a kind of collective leadership that is much more horizontal than vertical. Social innovators Peter Senge, Hal Hamilton, and John Kania describe "collective leadership" as a kind of leadership that operates far more by coordination than command. Discovering, implementing, and experimenting with multiple solutions to multiple intersecting problems requires a lot of collaboration across many different types of institutions: governments, international organizations, the commercial and nonprofit sectors. Leading collectively keeps everyone collaborating across a complex system and yet also allows individual parts to take initiative and drive independently toward common goals. All of the leaders across the system share power, in the sense that they allow themselves to be coordinated and are willing to collaborate in a situation in which power will flow from the collective.

It will probably not surprise you to learn that leaders who succeed in keeping many other people who are also leaders on task and collaborating are comfortable in more horizontal relationships. These leaders work more by building trust and taking the time to develop relationships than exercising authority. They also listen hard and learn to "see reality through the eyes of people very different from themselves."[8] They can move back and forth between many roles themselves, with relatively little ego.

Grand historical figures like Nelson Mandela practiced this kind of collective leadership to build the kind of coalitions and movements necessary for global change. Nelson Mandelas do not come along very often, however, and our problems won't wait. We have to pool our resources and our power.

A final example of power that is both shared and distributed among many groups or organizations but still manages to get things done is just emerging, enabled by technology but unworkable without a deep dose of humanity. Indian entrepreneurs Nandan and Rohini Nilekani have developed something called the "societal platform," a technological platform that creates the environment and tools and brings together the resources—financial and technological—to allow people from all different sectors to "co-create" and experiment with solutions to big social problems. They explicitly rely on equal engagement of all participants under "distributed leadership." The jargon is daunting for the uninitiated, but let me provide one example where this approach is working at scale in the United States.

Project ECHO (Extension for Community Health Outcomes), sponsored by the American Academy of Pediatrics, is a platform that brings together doctors and other health care professionals with scientists and subject matter experts to identify and share pediatric best practices in an "all learn, all teach" approach. Participants "tele-mentor" individual doctors, often in small rural hospitals, who raise issues or questions they have about how to care for specific patients. Think of it as a virtual agricultural extension service, in which the farmers participate just as much as the experts, or as a way of recreating the doctors' rounds that take place at high-quality teaching hospitals, with contributions from many different specialists.

Patients treated by doctors who are participating in Project ECHO have the same or better outcomes as patients who are referred to specialized hospitals, at lower cost and with less disruption to patients' lives. Moreover, the approach is spreading, as ECHO participants train other organizations that then create their own extension hubs.

What is most striking about this approach is that the technology is only a tool to enable equal participation by "communities of learners" or "co-creators" who share ideas and expertise to generate hundreds or thousands of local solutions—patient by patient, school by school, township by township. It combines local autonomy with vast potential scale, much as the designers of American democracy hoped to do by creating a federal system.

———

It is alluring to imagine a more heterogeneous United States adopting more pluralist and equal modes of problem solving. A growing army of experimenters in civic organizations, policy labs, and government itself are starting with people rather than problems and asking those people what they think they need.[9] The answer from an unhoused person is not always a house; the answer from a poor person may be reliable transportation to a job; the answer from a mother may be a stable work schedule. Technology may help implement solutions, but the power to design them must be shared.

Let us not imagine utopia, however. As the U.S. federal experiment has repeatedly demonstrated, systems structured for collaboration can just as easily enable competition and rivalry. No design for the wielding of power, however ingenious, can fully compensate for human greed and ill will.

CHAPTER 6

Looking Backward and Forward

In the coming chapters, I will turn the telescope to focus less on the personal and more on the national. To explore what renewal can mean not just for me, but for you and for all of us, putting together some of the specific themes we have already explored.

As I've recounted, a crisis in 2017 pushed me into a process of personal renewal, a path that has been exhilarating, rewarding, and hard. It has meant running toward the criticism not only in the moment but also in terms of looking backward over parts of my life and finding negative patterns. It has required building a new kind of resilience by reaching out to others and finding larger purpose in our daily work, resilience that has helped me use some of the criticism I heard as an opportunity for change. It has led me to reassess the conditions under which I was and am willing to take risks and what then is necessary to encourage risk taking in others. It has changed the way I lead, or at least try to lead: as horizontally as possible, from the center *and* the margin. It has changed my understanding of how best to exercise power.

Through this process, because of New America's mission "to renew the promise of America" but much more urgently because of the miasma of hatred, racism, classism, division, lies, and fear spreading over the United States and many other countries, I have thought continually about national renewal. Is it possible, and what will it take, for the United States not to "become great again," but to regain and establish a collective sense of progress toward a set of grand and worthy goals? Can we renew our energies, our hope, our sense of possibility? Only if "our" comes to mean all of us, and if we can change individually as well as together. And only if we can find a way forward that does not leave our past behind.

I have defined renewal as a process of looking backward and forward at the same time. First the "re" part, as in redo: facing who you are and have been as honestly as possible, as measured by actions rather than intentions, acknowledging and, to the extent possible, repairing damage done and harm inflicted. Returning again and again, no matter how long it takes. Then the "new" part, bringing something into the world that does not yet exist: behaving in new and better ways, which requires finding things in yourself to be proud of and build on going forward. Through both parts of this process, it is necessary to believe in and commit to the possibility of real and lasting change.

Why renewal rather than reinvention? After all, looking backward has not been the American way. According to European American origin stories, America is the land of leaving the past behind. Generations of immigrants were either forced or chose to reinvent themselves and their lives in a new country. Even today, the burgeoning self-help sections of every bookstore promise "a whole new you" on every dimension possible, from diet to destiny. For young people particularly, still trying on different versions of themselves, the emphasis on looking backward to move forward seems odd and encumbering. Why not start completely fresh?

Because we can't. The older we get, the more we realize that we cannot simply shuck the past, no matter how little or much of it we have behind us. We are shaped by our history, personal or national, as surely as a tree is shaped by soil, sun, wind, and rain. We cannot avoid a reckoning. In the speech he gave in 1990 on "Personal Renewal," John Gardner told his audience: "The individual intent on self-renewal will have to deal with ghosts of the past—the memory of earlier failures, the remnants of childhood dramas and rebellions, accumulated grievances and resentments that have long outlived their cause."[1]

Most white Americans, but also some communities of color, must confront the ways that our forebears have created and entrenched racism, exclusion, and social injustice, as well as the ways that we ourselves have allowed those patterns to persist, with as much honesty as we can muster. Still, these encounters with the past can be our teachers. If we look back often enough, the way learning organizations continually conduct postmortems on things that have gone wrong, we gain insights that can crystallize into wisdom.

Because renewal is more forgiving than reinvention. Renewal demands the searing heat of honesty, yet finds something positive to renew. On the national level, this element of renewal may be the hardest pill to swallow for the many Americans who are deeply angry about the persistent, entrenched, and all too often deliberate inequalities that track lines of race, color, class, creed, gender, and sexual orientation in this country. Personally, however, self-hatred or unremitting self-criticism simply cannot be a foundation for change. Every therapy, every self-help philosophy, and most creeds or religions recognize the need for a measure of self-love and acceptance as the basis for starting over and recommitting to a course of behavior or a set of values.

As I look back and try to accept the full implications of the ugliest parts of our history, accepting that "this is also who we are" as a country, I can still take pride in so many Americans, sung and unsung, who believed in something far better than what they saw around them, who imagined a society that did not exist and dedicated themselves to bringing it about.[2] I can honor them even as I now understand that many of them fell far short of and even betrayed the ideals they fought for.[3] I am also proud that American ideals are so big and bold, even as they cause people in many countries to shake their heads and chuckle at our naivete. It is far easier to be cynical than sincere.

Because renewal can be perpetual. Consider the renewal of vows, something that many of us do individually and with one another. Our marriage vows, our professional pledges, our pinky swears, our New Year's resolutions. We recall and recommit to our best selves, believing that those best selves exist and can be summoned or tapped. We can do that every morning, every month, every moment when we find ourselves falling back into old habits and practices. Indeed, the choice I made to run toward the criticism and use what I heard as a lever for learning and change can become a reflex or muscle, one that will grow stronger with exercise until it is automatic.

The pursuit of American ideals, which U.S. leaders have often proclaimed as universal ideals, draws a line, often a bloody and brutal path, between Thomas Jefferson's Declaration of Independence, with a vision of a far more equal society for white men than England had ever allowed, to Martin Luther King Jr.'s description of the "magnificent words" of the Declaration and the Constitution as a "promissory note" on which "America has defaulted."[4] King's dream cannot be denied by his fellow Americans precisely because, as he explained, "it is deeply rooted in the American dream."

King went on to quote the Declaration of Independence and then the words of "My Country, 'Tis of Thee," with its refrain of "let freedom ring." He challenged all Americans to make their words, their speeches, their songs, actually ring *true*, and thereby to make America "a great nation." Not "great again," but great. Just as Langston Hughes implores his audience to "let America be America again," even as he says, as a Black man, "America was never America to me."

Over the sixty years of my lifetime, I have seen the line between King's speech at one end of the National Mall to Amanda Gorman's poem at the other. Speaking at President Biden's inauguration, the first national youth poet laureate performed a mesmerizing text titled "The Hill We Climb." It began by recognizing the United States as

> a nation that isn't broken
> but simply unfinished
> We the successors of a country and a time
> Where a skinny Black girl
> descended from slaves and raised by a single mother
> can dream of becoming president
> only to find herself reciting for one.[5]

That line is not a smooth line of progress; it has often been a zigzag of backlash and brutality. Yet it is a line that has seen the nation's first African American president and first lady, and now a woman vice president who is both African American and Asian American. The lesson of renewal, however—once again—is that, as Americans, we cannot allow ourselves to separate the progress from the pain.

———

Looking backward as a nation means retelling our history, not only by bringing in the voices of as many Americans as possible, but also by highlighting new strands. Chapter 7 retells some familiar slices of American history in a way that brings out the themes of resilient interdependence rather than rugged individualism. These themes have particular resonance for me, as I explain, but they are also a demonstration of the way in which Americans, or people of any nation, can not only confront their past but retell parts of it to highlight buried traits and traditions that they can build on.

Chapter 8 is a call to think and build big, a reminder that we have not only to look backward as honestly as we can, but also to look forward and lift our sights. I offer *my* vision of what the United States could look like in the coming decades, with examples of what is already happening. What is most important, however, is to bring Americans together with the promise of doing really big things, showing the world and ourselves what we are capable of.

As I have learned, we won't be able to move forward even five years, much less fifty, without a measure of grace, the subject of chapter 9. Chapter 10 imagines a nation in which we can be many and one at the same time, glorying in our diversity and yet unified by our common commitment to equality, justice, liberty, and democracy. A vision for Americans and for the peoples of many other nations. The coda offers a glimpse into one version of what 2026 could look like, a set of aspirations for the next five years that could launch fifty years of change.

Time for a very different history lesson.

CHAPTER 7

Rugged Interdependence

While the founding fathers were declaring independence, the founding mothers were practicing interdependence. The wives, mothers, and sisters of the nation's celebrated patriots and politicians—Abigail Adams, Mercy Otis Warren, Eliza Pinckney, Kitty Greene, Martha Washington, and many others—managed the farms, plantations, and businesses that the men in their lives left behind.[1] They relied on extended families, neighbors, indentured servants, and the enslaved workers many of them held as property to help see them through tough and frightening times.[2]

This contrast, and the complexities that underlie it, is just one of countless counternarratives to the stock American history so many of us learned growing up. I now understand that the American history I was taught in school is a set of carefully composed paintings where the pentimento is showing: earlier images that the artist tried to cover over in the original work but that reemerge as the paint grows thin. The past is a vast tangled skein of the intersecting lives of millions of people. The lives we choose to remember, the communities we choose to describe, the lenses of good and evil we choose to apply, all tell us as much about the present as the past. As new generations of historians who look very different from the grand white men of old emerge to do the choosing, people, events, and themes that were long invisible become visible.

I was an undergraduate when Natalie Zemon Davis, the first woman historian to be tenured at Princeton, pioneered the writing of "women's history," an account of what the other half of the human race was doing over the centuries of our collective past.[3] Howard Zinn published *A People's History of the United States* the year I graduated, bringing a Jewish working-class activist perspective to bear on who "the people" whose stories deserve to be told actually are and knocking European American heroes off pedestals left and right.[4] Many new histories have followed, pioneered by historians reflecting the kaleidoscope of American identities.[5]

Given that for centuries white men have been fascinated with the history of other white men, it is hardly surprising that scholars from other groups in the United States want to trace the doings of people with whom they can identify. To take only one example, one of Natalie Zemon Davis's colleagues at Princeton was Nell Irwin Painter, who deliberately wrote "across the color line" in writing Southern history. Painter brought us first a biography of Sojourner Truth and later a history of "white people," exploring whiteness the same way so many white anthropologists and historians have explored the race of others.[6]

American history must ultimately include the stories of all who consider themselves American, often stories of violence, bloodshed, burning, forced displacement, genocide, slavery, and conquest. That is what renewal requires. The people and events that I choose to highlight here reflect my own preoccupation with stories of resilience and common effort, stories that highlight the contributions of women and African Americans in particular. I believe that Americans can recover a tradition of our interdependence as much as our independence, of other-reliance as much as self-reliance, of belonging as much as setting forth for the frontier. That tradition can in turn underpin a future of connection and care.

White Americans have long looked at ourselves—our society and political system—in a mirror held up by a Frenchman. Alexis de Tocqueville traveled across the United States from 1831 to 1832, returning to France to publish, over a decade, his massive two-volume *Democracy in America*. Excerpts from Tocqueville dot the curriculum of every high school and college course in American history. His observations reinforce our ideal vision of ourselves while feeding our favorite myths: his opening sentence announces, "Among the new objects that attracted my attention during my stay in the United States, none struck my eye more vividly than the equality of conditions."[7]

Tocqueville describes a nation of equal, independent citizens, governing themselves through New England–style town halls within a federal system. Given the twin conditions of equality and independence, each of which, in his view, strengthened the other, the American way of getting things done was through "association." "Among the countries of the world," he writes, "America is . . . the one where they have taken most advantage of association and where they have applied that powerful mode of action to a greater diversity of objects."[8]

The desire to associate with others, in Tocqueville's view, is inextricably connected with individual autonomy and self-reliance. Thus, "the inhabitant of the United States learns from birth that he must rely on himself to struggle against the evils and obstacles of life," but also learns to use his individual power to associate with others and thereby achieve his goals. Americans come together for every purpose on earth: public security, business, worship, and charity. All these individuals learn that they can achieve anything by exercising their collective power.

It is striking here that independence and interdependence must go together; the more separate the individual, the more she needs to choose to come together with others to achieve common goals. But a woman traveling through the United States in the 1830s might also have observed a deep tradition of communal work. Today we still have "spelling bees," a holdover from an earlier era of "bees" for spinning, quilting, sewing, canning, and preserving—also husking, apple picking, or logging. The word is not connected to the insect, but rather to the Middle English word "bene," also the root of a favor or "boon." It was used in early America to describe "voluntary help given by neighbors toward the accomplishment of a particular task."[9]

These are traditions not of setting out alone but of coming together, relying on community and mutual assistance. Tocqueville wrote mostly about men—free white men—and even there he tells a rich story of cooperation and association, one that was often erased by later historians and politicians. Imagine how much community support he would have needed had he been a woman or an African, Latin American, or Asian traveling observer rather than an aristocratic Frenchman.

It would never have occurred to me to challenge these texts in college. Tocqueville is a classic, after all. Today, however, I would tell my sons and my nieces and nephews to read history as much for the stories that aren't being told as those that are, and to ask why. Even if I think about the history of my family over my lifetime, each of my brothers and I would undoubtedly highlight quite different strands of stories that we all remember, putting the teller in the best light. History unavoidably depends on who is doing the telling.

Ralph Waldo Emerson's essay "Self-Reliance," written in 1841, is another staple of the history of American thought, read by high school and college students for generations. But while Ralph Waldo was preaching self-reliance as the transcendentalist creed, his wife Lidian observed that as far as she could see, the transcendentalists relied quite a bit on their wives and servants. In a short satire titled "Transcendental Bible," she pointed out all the ways in which the transcendentalists of her acquaintance welcomed in practice the things they scorned in theory (good dinners, nice clothes, comfortable houses—the material pleasures they purported to transcend).[10]

Ralph Waldo also famously preached nonconformism: "Whoso would be a man must be a nonconformist." "Trust thyself," he wrote, "every heart vibrates to that iron string." Self, self, self—the word recurs in every paragraph. "Insist on yourself, never imitate." "Nothing can bring you peace but yourself." "I must be myself."[11] Lidian, who held more orthodox and conservative religious views than her husband, gently ridicules the importance of doing "your whole duty to your noble self-sustained, impeccable, infallible, Self."[12]

Beyond satire, however, it is also worth taking a deeper look at Ralph Waldo Emerson's concept of what the "self" we are to rely on actually *is*. When he wrote of "self-trust," he imagined a kind of innate self that each of us has and can rely on.[13] He is talking about spontaneity, instinct, intuition—something that all humans share.

Critically, this sense of being unites us with one another, with nature, and with a transcendent collective intelligence. "Self" reliance, from this vantage point, means something very different from libertarian independence or even bohemian nonconformism. We are instead finding common identity and purpose by allowing ourselves to access and rely on a higher self.[14]

Margaret Fuller, a pioneering feminist, journalist, educator, and critic who was an important member of the transcendentalist movement, made the point more directly. She wrote in her memoirs of a "mystical experience" she had as a young woman on Thanksgiving Day in 1831, when she left a church service to wander through the fields near her father's home in Massachusetts. She describes pausing beside a little stream and gazing into a dark pool, where she reflected on "How came I here? How is it that I seem to be this Margaret Fuller? What does it mean?"

As she sat and pondered, she had a transcendent experience, which she explains as being "taken up into God." "I saw that there was no self; that selfishness was all folly, and the result of circumstance; that it was only because I thought self real that I suffered; that I had only to live in the idea of the ALL, and all was mine."[15]

Seen from this vantage point, transcendentalism is really a form of American Buddhism, a reaching for and merging into a higher consciousness or universal being. That is a very different vision than the veneration of Emerson the iconoclast and Henry David Thoreau the solitary nature-lover, carving their own paths through the intellectual and physical wilderness. (In fact, Walden Pond was only two miles from Concord and Thoreau's mother regularly brought him dinner and did his laundry.)

The reason to examine these texts so closely is to see up close how myths can be made and remade, depending on the purposes of the myth-makers. Both interpretations capture a dimension of transcendentalism; these were men and women willing to challenge the conventions of their religion and society in a way that supports the creed of individualism, rugged or otherwise. But they also created a commune designed "to substitute a system of brotherly cooperation for one of selfish competition" and supported abolitionism on the grounds that "man is one, and that you cannot injure any member, without a sympathetic injury to all members."[16]

It is up to us, Americans today, to look back and lift up different aspects of our past, a collective past that is continually expanding as different groups have the opportunity to tell the stories of *their* ancestors. And as we do, it is easy to find strands of deep resilience supported by mutuality and solidarity: the ability to strike out on our own only because we have others with us.

Thoreau is often invoked as a guiding spirit for the great nineteenth-century pilgrimages of covered wagons—the schooners of the prairie—heading West. "Eastward I go only by force," he wrote, "but westward I go free. . . . We go westward as into the future, with a spirit of enterprise and adventure."[17] To the politicians and historians who championed the concept of "manifest destiny," those wagon trains were the engines of American expansion, driven by men determined to find their freedom and make their fortune by heading to the frontier.

The diaries of the travelers, many of them written by the equally intrepid women who made the journey, even though many if not most really didn't want to go, do sound the themes of grand adventure and higher purpose.[18] But they are also full of stories of mutual help. The wagons contained entire families, who depended completely on one another; the families of the multiple wagons in a train made up a larger interdependent society on the trail, sharing food, doctoring one another, repairing broken equipment, rounding up livestock, and defending against human and natural enemies. In the words of one chronicler, the pioneer hostility to authority reflects an ethos of "individualism and egotism," but on the trail itself, "collaboration and cooperation predominated over competition and narrow selfishness."[19]

So too, in many frontier settlements. Martha L. Smith described her family's move in search of "God's Country," from Missouri to Oklahoma to Texas to Oregon. Hers is a tale of homesteading and unremitting hard work, with plenty of community support through fires, famine, floods, sandstorms, and drought. Looking back, she reflected that she and her husband had "found just about every kind of person in every part of the country. We worked, made friends, helped out where we could and usually found that others were willing to help us when we had our troubles."[20]

I read these accounts of pioneering differently today than I would have when I was growing up in the 1960s and 1970s. Just as I turn back to the *Little House on the Prairie* series by Laura Ingalls Wilder, which I devoured as a girl, and realize how racist it is, I now read about "conquering the savages" and think of the massacres, betrayal, and ultimately genocide of Native Americans. I read about chopping through the dense roots of the prairie grasses to make sod houses, and the shooting of buffalo, prairie chickens, and passenger pigeons and think of the destruction of an extraordinary and beautiful ecosystem.

Yet I can still admire the persistence, determination, and sheer grit of these families who made their way across the country, forging new communities as they went. They personify resilient interdependence much more than rugged individualism, showing us a different face of history and different traditions to draw on.

━━━━━━━

The official name of the Chicago World's Fair of 1893 was the World's Columbian Exposition, to celebrate the four hundredth anniversary of the year Christopher Columbus "discovered" America, a verb and a story many Americans now reject or at least caveat. We presented ourselves to the world as a country of optimism, progress, and unshakable faith in technology. Author Erik Larson described the fair evocatively as a "dream city," one square mile with more than two hundred buildings that visitors entered somberly, "as if entering a great cathedral. Some wept at its beauty."[21] Less remembered is that journalist and activist Ida B. Wells joined with other African American leaders calling for a boycott of the exposition based on its exclusion of Black voices and negative depictions of the Black community.[22]

Inside the exposition, Frederick Jackson Turner—a historian of the age in which the men who wrote American history seem all to have had grand three-barreled names—gave his famous address "The Significance of the Frontier in American History."[23] He read it as a scholarly paper before the members of the American Historical Association, which was meeting at the fair. His argument had many facets, but the core is the idea that the repeated encounter with an ever-moving Western frontier forged the individualism of American character and of American democracy itself.[24]

Needless to say, he described a *male* character, more precisely a white male character. And what men they were! They combined "coarseness and strength . . . with acuteness and inquisitiveness." They were practical, inventive, masters of "material things" that they could use to achieve "great ends." They had a "restless, nervous energy," and the "buoyancy and exuberance which comes with freedom."[25]

Turner's analysis, though deeply revised and contested by historians since, may still hold in some ways as an explanation of the relative libertarianism of the American West, the resistance to governmental control of any kind. Yet at least to my eyes, what is most striking is the way he completely collapses American men and their families.

Turner *sees* the family; indeed, he observes, "Complex society is precipitated by the wilderness into a kind of primitive organization based on the family."[26] He describes the ways in which pioneers would strike out with their families and gather other families around to create rude settlements. It is the father who matters, however; family members are the baggage he drags with him on his great individualist adventure.

Yet as we have just seen, the accounts written by those family members tell a very different but parallel story, one of interdependence and, indeed, of greater equality between men and women.[27] What if the significance of the frontier in American history was that it reinforced the lesson, over and over again, of the necessity of nurturing and supporting strong family and community bonds, without which individuals cannot survive?[28]

For this very different vision of American society, we need travel barely nine miles from where Turner lectured his audience at the exposition, to the site of Hull House. There, the activist and social reformer Jane Addams, a slight woman with "luminescent eyes and a determined tilt to her chin," had found her calling.[29]

In 1887, Addams read a magazine article about Toynbee Hall in London, a "settlement house" founded in East London as part of the Settlement Movement, which aimed to bring middle-class "settlers" to live together in working-class districts, to share knowledge and culture and build community. As patronizing and classist as it may sound today, these were a different breed of settlers, trying to advance reform and progress by crossing social rather than natural boundaries.

Two years later, Addams and her friend Ellen Gates Starr founded Hull House, in a donated building standing between an undertaker and a saloon in an almost entirely immigrant neighborhood in Chicago. The settlement gradually expanded to thirteen buildings—classrooms, auditoriums, gymnasiums, a day care center, and communal living and dining facilities. They differed from their British counterparts in the Settlement Movement by focusing specifically on recent immigrants, which in Chicago at that time meant immigrants from many different parts of Europe. Of Chicago's roughly one million inhabitants in the late 1890s, an astonishing 78 percent were either first- or second-generation immigrants.[30]

Addams believed in the importance of reciprocal relationships and common intercourse in building a shared civic life.[31] Reciprocity, the willingness to take as well as give, to acknowledge need in oneself as well as identify it in others, thereby opening the door to mutual vulnerability, is a critical step toward true interdependence.

Turner and Addams reflect two very different stereotypical conceptions of the American "character": male and female, grand and domestic, solitary and cooperative, rugged and reciprocal. They also envisioned very different frontiers: physical versus social. The coming twentieth century would develop an entire genre of movies dedicated to the myth of the lonesome and self-reliant cowboy, but it would also recognize that a modern economy and society had to be based on reciprocal rights and duties, at least for some Americans.

As I read these contrasting texts, I think about Gilligan and her concepts of the ladder and the web, an ethic of justice versus an ethic of care. I wonder how Americans and the world would think about the United States if women, African Americans, and the many other different ethnic groups that comprise our population had written our history. I wonder if I, as a girl and then a young woman learning that history, might have imagined my own role in America's future differently.

Fast-forward thirty-five years from 1893 to 1928, a year before the "roaring twenties" would crash into the economic crisis that became the Great Depression. It was an age of expanded individual freedom, particularly for women, and for many African Americans who headed North from the Jim Crow South in the Great Migration. It was also the first decade after the Russian Revolution, a post–World War I world in which communists in the new Soviet Union and socialists in Europe and the United States imagined a very different social contract between government and citizens, setting up a political competition that would dominate the twentieth century.

Herbert Hoover wrote a book in 1922 titled *American Individualism*.[32] In 1928, as the Republican candidate for president, he added the adjective "rugged," weaving a new strand into the American creed. In his acceptance speech at the Republican Convention in West Branch, Iowa, he described "our fathers and grandfathers who poured over the Midwest" as "self-reliant, rugged, God-fearing people of indomitable courage."[33]

They forged the "American system of rugged individualism," a system that Hoover saw as America's national task to preserve, as opposed to flabby European collectivism. In his view, government's job was to be a referee or umpire, restraining domination or abuse of power and ensuring fair play, but never to interfere with property rights or to use economic power for the common good.[34]

Four years later, after Hoovervilles and Hoover flags (empty turned-out pockets) had become national watchwords to describe the misery caused by the ballooning Depression, a very different presidential candidate gave a very different campaign speech at the Commonwealth Club in San Francisco. Franklin Delano Roosevelt called for rewriting "the old social contract" to enable government to check the power of corporate oligarchs and maintain a balance sufficient to allow individual citizens to find safety and opportunity.[35]

As it turned out, Roosevelt and his fellow New Dealers rewrote that contract in ways that deliberately excluded the majority of African Americans from programs like Social Security, meaning that tens of millions of Americans still struggle to find safety and opportunity, a legacy that must be considered in assessments of the New Deal. His mutualism had its limits—if not personal, then political. He nevertheless created much of the foundation of interdependence on which subsequent generations of reformers have built.

For both Roosevelt and Hoover, individualism and interdependence were not mutually exclusive. Roosevelt certainly believed in individualism, which he described as "the watchword of American life" in the nineteenth century, a time he described as one of permanent opportunity guaranteed by the open frontier. Hoover, for his part, believed deeply in mutuality. In his paeans to our "rugged" American forebears, he described the ways in which they "combined to build the roads, bridges, and towns; they cooperated together to erect their schools, their churches, and to raise their barns and harvest their fields." Indeed, he believed that "the quality of neighborly cooperation and mutual service" was as deeply embedded in the American character as self-reliance and initiative.[36]

They differed, of course, over the role of government, a difference that has been distorted and caricatured in ways that have helped lock American politics into our current polarities. In this wildly oversimplified story, Hoover stands for a libertarian laissez-faire tradition, while Roosevelt represents the nanny state. Each side invokes its own history.

Suppose that we came together and shared a common story, a story of *both* individualism and mutuality. A story of individuals who are enabled to achieve their personal dreams and ambitions by the assurance that they are not alone, that they are both independent and interdependent, and as they give, so shall they receive. A story with the message that the reciprocal ties of family, however we define it, and community, wherever we find it, is as fundamental an element of the American character as individual striving.

By midcentury, a great American prophet would lift up this vision with a new text.

On a sweltering summer day in 1963, Martin Luther King Jr. stood at the top of the steps of the Lincoln Memorial, with the great statue of Abraham Lincoln behind him, and looked out at hundreds of thousands of men and women who had marched on Washington to gather on the Mall. In words that are as powerful and moving as the Gettysburg Address, he reaffirmed the ideals of the Declaration of Independence. "I have a dream," he thundered, "that one day this nation will rise up, live out the true meaning of its creed: 'We hold these truths to be self-evident, that all men are created equal.'"[37]

But King's was a declaration of interdependence far more than of independence. Not only the interdependence of the African American community, marching and resisting side by side and arm in arm, but also the interdependence of the white and Black communities. King urges the Black members of his audience to recognize and trust the white people standing beside them, white people who "have come to realize that their destiny is tied up with our destiny . . . that their freedom is inextricably bound up with our freedom."

Here King is reaffirming the creed of mutuality, which he distilled in his equally famous "Letter from a Birmingham Jail," written just four months earlier. He wrote to respond to a public statement issued on Good Friday by eight local white clergymen who essentially accused him of being an outside agitator bringing trouble to Birmingham. He wrote of "the interrelatedness of all communities and states," explaining that he could not sit in Atlanta and ignore events in Alabama. He continued, in one of his most quoted passages:

> Injustice anywhere is a threat to justice everywhere. We are caught in an inescapable network of mutuality, tied in a single garment of destiny. Whatever affects one directly, affects all indirectly.[38]

We—the whole American people—can situate this creed in a different tributary of our collective past. White American history, at least the stylized version, looks back on the nineteenth century largely as a journey from East to West, the fulfillment of America's "manifest destiny" to spread out across the entire continent. Black American history is much more likely to focus on a different journey, one from South to North, not in covered wagons but on the Underground Railroad, and later in the Great Migration.

That journey has been made far more vivid in recent years through fiction, most notably Colson Whitehead's Pulitzer Prize–winning novel *The Underground Railroad*, but also Ta-Nehisi Coates's *The Water Dancer*. Ava DuVernay's movie *Harriet* similarly dramatized the life of Harriet Tubman as a conductor on the Railroad, a small, fiercely determined woman leading group after group of enslaved men, women, and children to safety, depending on the bravery and secrecy of fellow citizens willing to shelter them on the way North.

In Colson Whitehead's imagining, Cora, an enslaved woman who finally escapes from Georgia to a farm owned by a freeman in Indiana, watches a "shucking bee" at harvest time, in which two groups of farmhands race to shuck two enormous piles of corn the fastest. They sing a work song that Cora remembers from the plantation, leading her to wonder "how could such a bitter thing become a means of pleasure?" She sees that "work needn't be suffering, it could unite folks," that children can thrive and grow with the love of their parents, that they can achieve their dreams. "In her Georgia misery she had pictured freedom, and it had not looked like this. Freedom was a community laboring for something lovely and rare."[39]

Freedom as *community*. How starkly different from so many traditional American depictions of liberty as the freedom of a man—or a woman—to strike out on his or her own as an individual, to separate from the group and achieve independent goals. Here is a vision of freedom and unity, of liberty and love.

The Declaration of Independence is an assertion and justification of separation, of the need of a group of people, a nascent nation, to stand apart and define a distinct destiny. A Declaration of Interdependence is a recognition of what it takes to get there. It is an affirmation of a different set of truths: that only the most powerful and the most fortunate can achieve their goals seemingly alone, and even then, only by ignoring the visible or invisible help they received along the way.

Both are true. The recognition of both will make us a far stronger and more resilient nation. The new histories are designed to include, not exclude, to expand rather than contract a common past. "Both/and" is a far better approach than "either/or."

Pick up any book of American "tall tales," or browse through the nearly thousand pages of Benjamin Botkin's *A Treasury of American Folklore: Stories, Ballads, and Traditions of the People*, first published in 1944 with a foreword by Carl Sandburg.[40] The transformation of the faces of America in the intervening three-quarters of a century has been dramatic. Still, as the nation approaches the 250th anniversary of July 4, 1776, the distillation of our first 150 years in that anthology is instructive.

You will find in its pages, over and over again, stories of a nation of white men: bold adventurers all, subduing fearsome wild animals and conquering the frontier. They are tales of American folk heroes, from Davy Crockett to Pecos Bill and Paul Bunyan. Indeed, Botkin subdivides his compendium into many parts, the first of which is titled "Heroes and Boasters," with the following subcategories: "Backwoods Boasters," "Pseudo Bad Men," "Killers," "Free Lances," "Miracle Men," and finally, "Patron Saints," a very small section that includes the story of George Washington and the cherry tree, three tales of "Honest Abe" Lincoln, and one of Johnny Appleseed.

Only toward the end of the collection do a few voices of women, Indians, and Negroes—using the language of the time—emerge. Similarly, the sixth edition of *The American Intellectual Tradition*, published in 2011, includes only a smattering of writings from women and African Americans, mostly from the second half of the twentieth century.[41] It omits voices from any other race or ethnicity, few Jewish voices, and none from any other religion, with other kinds of diversity not even acknowledged.

My point here is not to be "politically correct," a pejorative label that American politics would be better off without. It is to point out how much richer, deeper, and stronger our collective roots would be if we could increasingly tell and hear *all* our stories as a nation, both because diversity brings a wide range of talents and strengths and because so many of those untold stories are stories not of victory but of resilience. They are the stories of minorities, of people forced to accept their subordinate role in society even amid the freedoms of the frontier. They are, thus, often stories both of suffering and survival and also of solidarity and strength.

In *More than Ready*, Cecilia observes that "pretty much by definition, [women of color] are at most only a few generations removed from people who showed extraordinary resilience and strength and who endured what seems unendurable. Our ancestors were survivors and strivers, generation after generation."[42] Bryan Stevenson says: "We can create communities in this country where people are less burdened by our history of racial inequality. The more we understand the depth of that suffering, the more we understand the power of people to cope and overcome and survive."[43]

I grew up reading all-male American tall tales and absorbed at least some of the ideal of heroic individualism embedded in them, even as a girl. They were all-white stories, so perhaps I would have felt differently if I had been a Black or Latina girl. My point, however, is that all of literature assumes that we can suspend our sense of self enough to identify with and learn from others who are very different from us. I certainly would not want to be confined to a world in which I read stories told only by or about people who look just like me. Yet neither would I want a world much closer to the one I grew up in, in which most stories and histories were told by and about people who do not look like me.

Similarly, to say rugged individualism is a myth is not to say that it is not part of the "American character." It is to say that the idea of the American character, or indeed of the "soul of America," is something that people construct for a variety of purposes, as Herbert Hoover did.[44] It is equally available to us—any of us, whether historian, politician, novelist, or activist—to pull different strands out of American history and make new myths, myths that are designed to inspire and guide coming generations of Americans in new directions.

I suggest that we tell tales of resilience and solidarity, as I have begun to do here, thereby highlighting people and communities too often left in the shadows. Resilience is necessary for renewal: the capacity to withstand and to transform. At the outset of the 2020s the nation faces a global pandemic, systemic racism and injustice, deep poverty and functional illiteracy, and continuing economic turbulence due to loss of jobs and technological transition. We will need all the resilience we can get.

At the same time, these stories will remind us of our collective ability to leap forward, to produce and follow leaders with bold and even seemingly impossible visions of what the future could be. We are capable of great things as a nation, all the greater when every member of the nation is engaged and heard. It is time to free our imaginations of all the cynical certainties as to why all the really big things we might want to do cannot be done, and allow ourselves to dream and do.

CHAPTER 8

Building Big

Big ideas excite me. They actually make my heart race. I feel a moment of transcendence, a path to a place in my head where I can see a vision of something truly new. I started looking for ideas about renewal in the work of the American transcendentalists several years ago, when it occurred to me that they were writing at the end of the first stage of the Industrial Age, from roughly 1830 to 1850, after steam and mass production but before electricity. They were looking for something more than machines: a celebration of land, nature, spirituality. I predict a similar movement in the coming decade as many people begin to rebel against the "second machine age," which is actually just the first stage of another vast technological transformation.[1]

Above all, according to the great scholar of transcendentalism Lawrence Buell, the men and women who came together in New England in the decades before the Civil War wanted to *create*. To create not just art, although many of them also wrote poetry and other forms of creative prose, but visions of what could be. "They were more excited by the vision and experience of the *process* of transformation" than by the actual implementation of their ideas.[2]

Today the literature on innovation is full of books and podcasts debunking the necessity and even the value of big ideas, arguing instead for the importance of little ideas that build on one another.[3] Fair enough; these authors are updating variations on Thomas Edison's famous saying that "Genius is one percent inspiration and ninety-nine percent perspiration," which, unlike many such quotations, can actually be traced back to Edison.[4] Still, human beings *need* inspiration. Many great historical figures, religious and secular, have been visionaries, even if some of their visions were dark and ultimately deadly. Great speeches, music, poetry, painting, and other works of art lift us to another plane. Think of the brevity and soul-stirring power of the Gettysburg Address.

I emphasize the point because in political terms, renewal offers a path forward that is far bolder than reform but short of revolution, a path of "non-reformist reforms."[5] Now is no time for incrementalism, but for change big enough to capture imaginations and change minds. California congressman Ro Khanna, who represents Silicon Valley and embraces deeply progressive politics, has argued for a left-wing politics of inspiration. "People don't just want a $15 minimum wage and healthcare and education," he explains. "They want a shot at doing amazing, big things, and we have to speak to that."[6] It is striking that Dr. King spoke of his "audacious faith in the future of mankind" when accepting the Nobel Peace Prize; forty-two years later, Barack Obama wrote of the "audacity of hope." I like to think of the "audacity of renewal."

In that spirit, I will outline a few of the changes that Americans could make, if we can gather the courage and the will, to renew our political, economic, and social systems. We have discussed others in earlier chapters. These are by no means exclusive; I could write a whole chapter on ways to overhaul our education system, from cradle to grave. I have selected the proposals below—to create a multi-party democracy in the United States, to support a whole new generation of American entrepreneurs, and to rethink the foundations of capitalism itself—because they exemplify the scale of the thinking we need and are already underway in some places. I encourage you to add your own visions of what could be, ignoring the naysayers and remembering all the great changes Americans and people around the world have been able to achieve when they got mad enough and determined enough.

When I was growing up as a girl in Virginia, it would never have occurred to me to think about running for office, even though my best friend's father had run for governor and politics was a frequent subject of conversation at my family's dinner table. Girls simply didn't do that sort of thing. In my forties and fifties, however, when I started giving frequent speeches to large audiences and responding to questions on everything from gender equality to foreign policy, people would periodically ask me if I had thought about running.

My answer was always the same. If I lived in England, I would say, where election campaigns are five weeks long, with strict spending limits and a ban on political advertising, I would run in a minute. In the American system, however, where members of Congress never *stop* campaigning to be elected or reelected every two years, campaigns for all other offices start years ahead of the actual election, and all campaigns require candidates to spend the majority of their time "dialing for dollars" from corporations and multimillionaires, no chance.

Think about that answer. Not because our system deters *me*, but because of the thousands or tens of thousands of potential candidates, from every conceivable constituency in the country, who reason the same way and avoid politics. Furthermore, even winning candidates complain regularly about the need to continue fundraising even in office and the corruption that breeds, and now the relentless partisanship that makes it almost impossible to govern effectively at the federal level and in many statehouses as well. Finally, gerrymandering by parties in power in state legislatures turn many congressional districts into artificially safe seats and a winner-take-all electoral system gives candidates no incentive to appeal to a broad spectrum of voters across a state or the nation.

Americans *know* that our system is broken. Yet to remove any of these obstacles requires legislation that cannot pass precisely because our system is broken. Still, in the fall of 2019, with the hyperpolarization of American politics on daily display in the efforts of the House of Representatives to impeach Donald Trump, political scientist Lee Drutman predicted a "new age of reform and renewal ahead" for American democracy.[7] It cannot come soon enough.

Think big. Imagine a political system that actually represents the full spectrum of the American people. Imagine what it would feel like to be able to vote for congressional candidates who would have incentives to reflect the views of multiple slices of the electorate, rather than energizing "their base." To know that every election is actually a fair fight,[8] rather than a contest in which the rules have been rigged to favor the party in power. To elect governments that would get things done and keep them done in line with the desires and preferences of a majority of the American people.[9] Governments that would champion and secure the right of every citizen to vote.

Lots of reforms are possible—ending gerrymandering, limiting money in politics, automatic voter registration, universal vote-by-mail—but it's time for much bolder action. The *one* change that could unlock the door to a cascade of others is to end the two-party duopoly and create a multi-party democracy.

Nothing in the Constitution dooms us to an eternal war between Democrats and Republicans, or any other two parties. Quite the contrary, the framers naively assumed that parties would fade away. It is the two parties themselves, as they have evolved, that have created a "political-industrial complex,"[10] a "doom loop" that makes polarization and paralysis steadily worse.[11]

We don't want an infinite number of parties: somewhere between four and six probably makes the most sense, just as we had de facto for most of the twentieth century, with liberal Democrats, conservative Democrats, liberal Republicans, and conservative Republicans. Perhaps a Libertarian party and a Green party would also emerge, although all parties would have to pass some kind of credibility threshold.[12] What is critical is to create a system in which voters who are dissatisfied with the positions or candidates of the two main parties can create a new party that better reflects their views, without their candidate becoming a spoiler. We also want to ensure that candidates have a chance to appeal to voters directly in a primary. With open primaries, the ability to rank our preferred candidates, instead of choosing just one, and instant runoffs, we can ensure that the candidate who wins actually gets a majority of the votes cast, rather than winning only 30 or 40 percent of the electorate but still a sliver more than the other candidate.

All of this is not only possible; it's happening. Both Maine and Alaska have voted to adopt instant runoff voting (also called ranked-choice voting) in federal and some or all state elections, as have more than twenty American cities.[13] Both are states that typically send independent or Republican candidates to the Senate. Campaigns are building to put this kind of voting on the ballot in multiple other states in different regions of the country.

At the national level, Americans have come together to overhaul our system before: to give African Americans the vote (twice, in the Fifteenth Amendment and the Voting Rights Act of 1965), to give women the vote, to strengthen the voting rights of Native Americans, to elect senators by direct election rather than through state legislatures, to allow primaries and referenda in addition to conventions, to change the voting age. The cry of reformers today is "more voices, more choices."[14] As we become a plurality nation, that is exactly what we need.

We can do it again. We need to *believe* we can do it, and to find enough common purpose to come together to get it done.[15]

On Twitter, people identify themselves in all sorts of ways, reflecting their own conception of who they are and what they care about rather than through their official job titles. Many put their family identity first (mother, father, spouse), declare their passions (runner, hiker, cook, music lover), or describe what it is they actually do in the world that cuts across jobs and titles (connector, network builder, community weaver, strategist, problem solver, activist, even "information DJ").

The opening line of my own brief ID says "Patriot. Entrepreneur. Mother. Mentor. Thinker. Feminist." The rest of it identifies me as the CEO of New America and lists some of my previous positions. But those first six words capture dimensions of who I am and what I do in a way that a résumé never will.

We'll come back to "Patriot." I want to focus now on "Entrepreneur," a title I have given myself. It has taken decades for me to realize that what I love most in the world is making things happen—through connecting people, creating new ideas and institutions, and catalyzing action. But I love doing those things my own way, following my own path, setting my own agenda—preferably now with a great team around me.

After spending a lot of time on the West Coast over the past decade, it gradually came home to me that I had more in common with many of the young people launching start-ups in Silicon Valley, Seattle, and Los Angeles than with many of my colleagues on the East Coast—the academics, policy experts, and government officials that were my community for decades. I admire my colleagues' commitment to the life of the mind, to public service, and to doing the often selfless work necessary to make large institutions work. But I identify more with people who are bringing something new into the world by building things: companies, organizations, and institutions.

I have come to understand that the quality of wanting not only to think but to do, not only to imagine but to build, is the essence of entrepreneurship. "Entrepreneur" is a funny word. The literal translation from the French is someone who undertakes, but "undertaker" obviously has a very different meaning in English. An entrepreneur is someone who undertakes to do something, to make something happen in the world, to create something where nothing existed before.

I became a full-fledged entrepreneur when I became CEO of New America at age fifty-five. Founded in 1999, by 2013 New America was having a messy adolescence. It was (and is) a community of brilliant people committed to improving the world, but as an organization it needed to be reformed and reinvented in any number of ways.

Looking back, I could write the same kind of book about building a team, heading in the wrong direction, scrambling to stay afloat, and taking advantage of unexpected good fortune as any Silicon Valley founder (although we play for very different stakes). Thinking about my role this way, as an entrepreneur as much as an organizational leader, has more accurately captured the type of work I do and given me more of a community.

I tell this story because I don't look like the media or Hollywood stereotype of an entrepreneur: a young man, usually white but occasionally brown, headed to California or sometimes New York to make his fortune with a big idea and a small team. Suppose we begin from a different presumption of what an entrepreneur looks like, one that would actually allow us to see entrepreneurs everywhere. In Kathryn Finney's tech incubators for Black and Hispanic women in Atlanta and Newark.[16] In the Latina Entrepreneur Academy, operating in sites across the country.[17] In small and medium-sized businesses across the country, many of which simply need more secure financing and ecosystem support to thrive.

Prior to the pandemic, research by the Kauffman Foundation found that more than 60 percent of Americans have a "dream business" they would like to create; some 40 percent say they would leave their current jobs to make that dream real if they had the financial backing and other kinds of support. That's easier to say than to do, but even if those numbers are inflated, the potential for a huge wave of entrepreneurship exists, particularly among women, minorities, and rural residents, all of whom are underrepresented in the business community generally and particularly in the start-up world.[18]

Mid- and postpandemic, with Main Street restaurants and retail businesses shuttering across the country, backing a new generation of entrepreneurs that reflects the demography of their communities to launch businesses and social enterprises will be an essential part of building a new American economy. Beyond financial benefits, this approach allows individuals, together with their families and communities, to shape their own futures, meeting local needs while taking advantage of a national tech infrastructure.[19] These entrepreneurs can also be the founders of a new green and clean economy, the renewable and sustainable economy that the United States and all countries need to ensure that we can continue to live on our planet. The objections are legion. Here is a sampling: the small local farms that have begun supplying food directly to residents and to restaurants for takeout during the pandemic will never be able to compete economically with industrial farms and big chain supermarkets; additive manufacturing (3-D manufacturing) cannot scale beyond makerspaces and university labs; telework and telemedicine will always be inferior to face-to-face interaction; young people will always want to flock to cities. Et cetera, et cetera.

Suppose, however, that the farm subsidies that now go overwhelmingly to massive agribusinesses were redirected to local farms, to serve the multiple goals of supply-chain resilience in the face of future pandemics and other disasters, nutritional needs in local schools, avoiding food deserts in poor communities, and reducing the climate impact of industrial farming. That is agricultural, educational, poverty, climate, and security policy all at once.

Suppose that as knowledge workers emerge from the pandemic, they want to get out of their homes but not into their cars, creating a demand for local coworking spaces that can support multiple business needs and a surrounding restaurant and small retail economy. Suppose we move to a kind of hybrid economy, combining the advantages of high-quality resources online with place-based quality of life. Suppose that the country moves to a six-hour workday, freeing up much more time for care and creative work of many different kinds, all of which can again draw on the power of digital learning and dissemination but can also reinvigorate a local arts scene.

All these things *could* happen. But not in an election cycle. Indeed, not in a generation. Perhaps in two generations, however. Social entrepreneur Sascha Haselmayer, who built a company to revolutionize public procurement in cities, explains that most public innovations take thirty years to crystallize and spread.[20] The citizens of Amsterdam invented public bike sharing in 1965; in 1998 the first companies entered the market; today, when bike sharing is finally becoming ubiquitous in cities around the world, the top five bike-share companies have all been launched since 2009.[21]

If we think big and build slow, organizing and funding for a much longer term than most movements, institutions, and foundations typically envision and using technology and learning platforms to engage as many people as possible as easily as possible, then all sorts of big changes could actually happen. Instead of starting from our problems and trying to figure out how to solve them, leaders of all kinds, including you, can invite our fellow Americans—or the citizens of your country—to think about what they really *want*, even if they think they can't have it. The next step is to figure out how to support a new generation of entrepreneurs to bring new ideas, institutions, and industries to life.

Suppose we could change the foundations of capitalism itself, at least of American-style capitalism. All sorts of "reinventing capitalism" initiatives are underway: the *Financial Times*, one of the world's premier business newspapers, is calling for a "better form of capitalism"; the U.S. Business Roundtable has come out in favor of "stakeholder capitalism" in lieu of "shareholder capitalism"; the Omidyar Network and the Hewlett Foundation are supporting ongoing work to generate new models of political economy beyond neoliberalism and to "reimagine capitalism";

and the Stanford Center for Advanced Study in the Behavioral Sciences has created a framework for a "new moral political economy."[22] I will not attempt to parse definitions of capitalism, distinctions between different versions of capitalism, and alternative doctrines like democratic socialism here; my point is simply that an intellectual ferment regarding the nature of capitalism is already underway in the United States and Great Britain, one that is also tied to large social movements like the Movement for Black Lives.

From my own perspective, the biggest problem with the American economic system—whatever label you put on it—is that it is based on half human beings. The traditional discipline and practice of economics assumes that humans are motivated only by the pursuit of rational self-interest, leading them to compete, and periodically cooperate, with other humans to achieve those interests. The name for this artificial creature is *Homo economicus,* a Latin name that designates a particular version of *Homo sapiens.* In recent decades, behavioral psychologists have systematically demonstrated, through ingenious experiments, the limits to human rationality, such that the subdiscipline of behavioral economics now assumes a kind *Homo psycho-economicus*—a human whose reason is bounded and distorted by a set of biases.[23]

Scholars in many other disciplines—sociology, anthropology, history, and now neuroscience—start from a very different image of humankind, one that begins from the proposition that humans are deeply social beings. I am skating over an entire library of books and articles here, from Aristotle to the present, debating the elements of human nature.[24] The key point, however, is that social beings have a fundamental need to connect to other human beings, to be embedded in relationships, and to belong to groups, from families to tribes to nations.

Connection, in this view, is as important and as life-sustaining as a full belly. It is an end in itself, not just a means to an end, and therefore drives human outcomes just as much as competition does.

Imagine if the basic image of a human being, the unit of analysis that underpins disciplines such as economics, law (which continually begins from the assumption of "the reasonable man"), politics, and philosophy, was whole people, people who have the full range of human emotions and desires. We could replace *homo economicus* with *sapiens integra*, a being who finds happiness and well-being not only as a function of her or his individual state, but of the state of others to whom she or he is connected. Most of us know that to be true in our own lives; it is a cliché among parents to say, "you are only as happy as your unhappiest child." Why should we build theories of the economy based on a caricature?

Big ideas for building new economic and social systems based on human connection abound. British designer Hilary Cottam has developed a social practice based on building connection, tackling problems from health care to chronic unemployment, and has written an entire manifesto for a social revolution based on *sapiens integra*.[25] Kate Raworth, an economist at Oxford University, has invented the idea of "doughnut economics" to allow humans to connect to the earth and one another in ways that will allow us to live sustainably within planetary limits.[26] Margaret Levi's continued exploration of "communities of fate" as a key dimension of a new moral political economy focuses on our relationships to "those, beyond our families, with whom we feel entangled, whose interests and welfare we perceive as tied to our own."[27] Finally, the argument for an infrastructure of care, discussed earlier, pioneered by activist and organizer Ai-Jen Poo, who has devoted her life to bringing it about, is now at the center of a whole community of thinkers, activists, businesswomen, policy entrepreneurs, and funders. All of us envision a society in which human connection to and investment in others is as valued as, say, money management and investment in real estate.[28]

Another aspect of a deeply different perspective on capitalism comes from an effort to fight the gospel of endless growth, the eternal search for *more*. No matter how big you get, how much money or market share you have, more is always waiting just around the corner. Venture capitalists are always looking for the next "unicorn," that rare start-up that scales to a $1 billion valuation before it goes public and vastly enriches its investors.

The alternative to a unicorn company is a zebra. In March 2018, four women entrepreneurs wrote a Medium post titled "Zebras Fix What Unicorns Break."[29] Where unicorns are bent on profiting from disruption, regardless of the social consequences, zebra companies are "both black and white: they are profitable *and* improve society." They seek "sustainable prosperity" instead of exponential growth, enough profit for the business to maintain itself and benefit its employees and the community. Investors should expect to receive double their initial investment, not the 10x that venture capitalists typically hope for.[30]

As of 2020, the Zebras Unite movement set its sights on reimagining business altogether, focusing on creating sustainable commercial enterprises that will share both profits and power with workers, users, and communities.[31] These Zebra companies are structured differently and are subject to different legal obligations than traditional for-profit corporations. Zebras, public benefit corporations, new kinds of cooperatives, and social enterprises are all examples of yoking the profit motive and a social motive together, to achieve enough profit to be

sustainable at a comfortable level and enough benefit to be socially valuable.

In finance, the investment group Springbank Collective seeks
to mobilize one hundred million dollars to close the gender gap.
Its founders have committed to sharing one third of Springbank's profits with nonprofit partners that work on gender policy and other systems change.[32] These examples are all rejections
of *more* in favor of *enough*.

In closing this chapter, I want to speak particularly to my generation of women—boomers and older Gen Xers. If we take the
generation of women born between 1950 and 1970—who are
just entering their fifties, sixties, and seventies as I write this—
we have time, experience, and enough power to drive really big
change. We can join hands with the women just behind us who
do not have caregiving responsibilities and are ready to push.
Our millennial and Gen Z daughters or granddaughters must
help, learning from us but also making sure we are not hope-
lessly out of touch. My favorite line in Bernardine Evaristo's
novel *Girl, Woman, Other* is when fifteen-year-old Yazz tells her
mother, Amma, "feminism is so herd-like . . . to be honest, even
being a woman is passé these days."[33]

These younger women may be surprised to find that their
grandmothers are primed for action. Pat Mitchell, who has had
a fabulous career as a journalist, media executive, catalyst, and
connector, calls her generation of women dangerous. In her
memoir, *Becoming a Dangerous Woman*, she makes the case
quite simply. "At this time in my life, about to turn seventy-five,
I have nothing left to lose," she writes.[34]

Mitchell is writing specifically about "the truly dangerous
work of making the world a safer place for women and girls." She

is following in a long tradition. Forty-year-old Elizabeth Cady Stanton, a founder of the nineteenth-century American women's rights movement who had just had her sixth child, wrote in a letter to her fellow activist Susan B. Anthony, "You and I have the prospect of a long life. . . . We shall not be in our prime before 50, and after that we shall be good for 20 years at least."[35]

But back to our story. Contrast Stanton's attitude—we shall not be in our prime before fifty!—with the modern assumption that menopause is a "change of life" to be dreaded, managed, and treated. Historian Susan Mattern challenges this view, arguing that the whole concept of menopause as a medical issue is a constructed modern phenomenon.[36] She explores a long-standing evolutionary puzzle: men can reproduce at much older ages than women can, but women have longer lifespans. Thus older, post-reproductive women must serve some useful function for the survival of the species.

The traditional answer to this question is that even though older women can no longer bear children, they can raise them and transmit social norms and the accumulated wisdom of their society. Mothers with grandmothers in the picture had an evolutionary advantage in the foraging and gathering necessary to keeping families fed. Mattern goes beyond this thesis and argues that the transition to a life stage "of high productivity and zero reproductivity" for half the population has been a fundamental factor in human progress. Sounds right to me.

New York Times columnist Gail Collins has written another wonderful book focused on older women, titled, appropriately enough, *No Stopping Us Now*.[37] Many older women of sufficient means to provide for themselves think of later life not as retirement and certainly not as a postmenopausal desert, but as "phase three," the phase after child rearing or other kinds of caregiving. I think of phase three as phase free, a time to take risks and upset apple carts.

Once again, the "we" I think of when I think of older women is a privileged category. Sixteen percent of all American women older than sixty-five live in poverty, a rate that rises to roughly 25 percent for Black, Hispanic, and Native American women. *One in four.* Women who never married, a category that includes many LGBTQ people, are equally vulnerable; 26 percent live in poverty.

Women face higher rates of poverty than men as they age because they are still paid less than men and have less opportunity to build savings or accumulate any other kind of wealth. Their caregiving work often keeps them out of the wage market, yet they are not eligible for Social Security. Health care costs and domestic violence complete the picture.[38]

All the more reason for those of us who have the time, energy, and means to fight for the women who have not had our advantages. We are long-lived. We are past what Alicia Menendez calls "the likeability trap," which is another way of saying we care less and less what people think about us.[39] We are the fastest growing part of the U.S. workforce.[40] We are old enough to understand that we cannot reinvent completely, but young enough to believe we can still change. In short, we have the time, energy, commitment, and attitude to take on something big: to embrace complexity, upend hierarchy, and harness new understandings of power, anger, and truth.

So join me. Let's wear hats. Save the planet. Renew our politics. Claim our place in the sun, or at least the national conversation. Bridge our multiple identities. Find a way forward that moves out and across, rather than relentlessly up.

Let's listen to one another, cite one another, rely on one another, and take charge as much as we can. But let's embrace our fathers, brothers, husbands, and sons and work for a world that is equal, not exclusive. Let's devote the rest of our lives to building big.

CHAPTER 9

Giving and Finding Grace

I am a person of faith, even if I do not subscribe to any particular faith. I believe deeply in the human capacity to believe in something bigger than we are—whether that is God, nature, humanity, beauty, or the cosmos—and to act on that belief in ways that cannot be explained by rational calculations of self-interest. I am drawn to spiritual texts of many different faiths, and have recently read my way through the Bible, from beginning to end, over the course of two years.

Here again, Tyra has helped me. In liberal academia, God is not a frequent topic of conversation. Tyra, however, has no inhibitions about making clear, as she wrote in *Time* magazine in 2016, that she counts her relationship with God as one of her blessings.[1] My conversations with her about her faith and my own spiritual reflections created an open space for further exploration.

Through this process of reading and conversation I have found myself particularly drawn to the concept of grace. Christians define grace in many different ways; it is also a concept in the Hebrew Bible and in Islam. I will avoid theological disputation here and instead offer my own understanding: a quality of kindness, mercy, charity, even love, that is given rather than earned.

Some measure of grace is necessary for renewal, both personal and national. On the personal side, as we have discussed, the need for grace is easy to see. It is impossible to change without a measure of self-love and compassion. We must face the bad in ourselves, but still find some good to hold on to.

Grace at the national level is much more complex. I am *not* suggesting that people who have been on the receiving end of systemic racism and injustice for decades and centuries should simply extend grace to the perpetrators of that injustice, past and present. The nation needs what Michelle Alexander, author of *The New Jim Crow*, calls a "process of racial reckoning" in schools, neighborhoods, and communities across the land. That work—of educating ourselves, forging a common consciousness, and allying for change—falls on white people.[2]

I am, however, advocating some patience with the learning process, learning that is an indispensable part of renewal. Those Americans who want to undertake this work, who have finally been shocked into awareness of the deeply unjust reality that so many of our fellow Americans live with daily, do not need or merit praise. We are bound to stumble, however, and to make mistakes in trying to have difficult conversations or to overcome blind spots. I hope that those whom we unwittingly offend can give us enough grace to allow us to continue the journey.

If I look back even over three or four years, it is astonishing to me how my own lenses on the world have changed. I wince now when I recall commenting on the appearance of a young person who had radically changed their dress and hairstyle from what we would consider more traditionally feminine to more traditionally masculine, saying that I preferred their former looks.

In retrospect it is completely clear to me that as the CEO talking to a younger employee, I should not have commented on their appearance at all, but at the time, I was thinking of them as a young woman whom I had hired, promoted, and (I thought) even mentored a bit and I was talking more in the way I would with close mentees. I was also just surprised and spoke without thinking—something that still happens to all of us regardless of age or role.

I had no idea that they were actually exploring different gender roles, something that, as I look back with the lenses of the present, seems completely obvious but that was then much less in the public consciousness than it is today. As it happened, I offended them, understandably, and the story quickly made the rounds among some of the younger people at New America.

I only wish that the incident could have been a teachable moment for me, rather than a lasting black mark. Given the power disparity between them and me, I understand why they might have felt uncomfortable responding directly, and of course they were certainly under no obligation to discuss their private life. They might, however, have told me that my remark made them uncomfortable and allowed me to apologize.

Alternatively, someone who heard about the incident could have come and explained to me the larger context, which would have allowed me to understand and bridge to a culture very different from the one I grew up in. I was definitely in the wrong. Still, it was a thoughtless mistake, not an intended slight or even negligent indifference.

That's just one example of remarks that get made, missteps taken, misjudgments rendered, that happen among all people and particularly among people who come from different backgrounds and places in life who must try to find a way to live, study, work, and vote together. We find it so easy to think the worst of one another, quickly and furiously. Perhaps grace can allow us to find a balance between a necessary holding to account and a granting of a little latitude to be human, to stumble and fall short.

———

Grace has another meaning, one that is not about giving it to others but finding it for ourselves.

Another one of the people I had the pleasure of interviewing for New America's digital magazine on resilience was Vincent Stanley, director of philosophy for Patagonia, a billion-dollar company that makes clothing and equipment for outdoor recreation. His may be the coolest title in corporate America; it comes from his decades-long role as a custodian of Patagonia's distinctive culture of responsibility and from his commitment to focusing the company on larger questions of "aspiration and purpose."

One of Stanley's favorite quotations is from Norman Maclean, author of *A River Runs through It*: "It is natural for man to try to attain power without recovering grace."[3] When I asked him about it, he talked of the human desire to "bring agency to our lives, . . . to do things, . . . to make our mark."[4] So when we do things, we want to own them, and to take credit, even though we are also invariably indebted to other people and forces beyond our own agency.

Stanley insists that we strive always to keep perspective, to strike a balance between our own existence and something larger. Grace is that "something larger," something that "doesn't come from anywhere. It comes from the world, it comes from nature, it comes from God." It is the necessary counterbalance to self, however, and sometimes surrender of self is necessary to find it.

In the fall of 2015, my friend Debora Spar, who was then president of Barnard College, invited me to give the Barnard commencement address the following spring. I was delighted and deeply honored. As it turned out, however, many of the Barnard students were less pleased. Shortly after I was announced, a group of students and faculty protested and signed a petition in favor of having the novelist and essayist Chimamanda Ngozi Adichie as their speaker.

I chose to meet these protests head on in the text of my talk. I praised the act of protest as part of a great liberal arts critical tradition and made clear how much I admired Adichie's work (she was sitting on the stage behind me). I then took on what I saw as a central issue raised by their protests: the question "of who can speak for whom and what we should be speaking about."

The petition signed by the protesters had described me as a representative of "white corporate feminism," the feminism of "upper-middle-class, white, heterosexual women" who focus on their own problems getting to the top of the career ladder rather than on the problems of all women. I have never been in the corporate world, and had just published a book focused on elevating the value of care, an issue I chose precisely because it intersects the lives of almost all women and has not exactly been on the corporate agenda, so I pushed back a bit.

I acknowledged, however, that I am white and upper-middle-class. I forged on and posed the question: "So, does my identity mean I cannot speak for women who do not look or live like me?"

At this point one of the young women graduates sitting before me yelled out, "Yes!" I still smile thinking about it, remembering just how bold and determined she was. At the time, I acknowledged the response, but continued to try to answer what I really did see as a critically important question: the same question, I pointed out, "that has created the generational split among so many women with regard to Hillary Clinton's presidential campaign. Older women see her as breaking barriers for all women; many younger women focus more on her wealth and privilege than on her gender." I went on to explain why I believed that Hillary, or I, could speak for all women while recognizing the need to create much more room for those women to speak for themselves.

The details of my argument really don't matter now; all I can say is that I was sincere. I went on to talk about the importance of valuing care as much as competition and of the necessity of changing male gender roles just as much as we have changed female roles if we are ever to achieve real equality. I concluded by quoting Adichie's essay *We Should All Be Feminists*.[5] The audience applauded when I finished, but perhaps more loudly from the parents' section than from the students'.

I lost a friend over this incident, an old colleague who had a daughter in the graduating class and had emailed me several times before the graduation to say how pleased he was that I would be the speaker, but then broke off all communication afterward. Looking back, particularly in light of Hillary Clinton's loss in the 2016 election and the deep continuing appeal of Bernie Sanders to many college students, I realize that many members of my audience thought I was giving a Clinton campaign speech, which I certainly did not intend. Perhaps, ironically, they heard *me* appealing to identity politics; I wanted a woman president; they wanted a world remade.

Over the intervening years, I have come to understand that I was wrong. Of course I *can* speak for women who do not look or live like me: representative democracy and allyship depend on that proposition. But I and everyone who looks and lives like me have had far more chances to speak and be honored than those who do not. I also realize that I was doing exactly what many feminists of color have decried. I have spent decades pushing other women forward in various ways—my students, mentees, colleagues, and women I barely know but whom I suggest for jobs or prizes. Still, in this moment I did not—perhaps could not—see and accept that the counterpart to pushing others forward is stepping back yourself.

Today I would ask if both Chimamanda and I could speak, on the assumption that some number of graduates would want to hear me as well, and if not, then I would switch places and sit on the stage while she gave the address.

Ideally, we would have a world of both/and rather than either/or. In the many cases where a choice must be made, however, the only way forward is to be willing to cede power, cede honors, cede things that matter to us as individuals to secure a better result as a community and society. A result that, for many if not all of us, matters just as much.

That process of ceding, of moving over or stepping down, is an example of relinquishing that sense of agency, of the ability to control things and take credit for them, that Vincent Stanley spoke of. Being able to let it go, to strike a balance with that vast starry space beyond us, is finding grace.

The choice to give grace is up to those who are injured, or suffering, or long oppressed. It is grace precisely because it is freely given. Still, for the sake of healing and moving forward as a country, I truly hope that we can embrace what Loretta J. Ross describes as a culture of "calling in" rather than "calling out."[6] Ross is a longtime reproductive rights activist, a Black feminist, a public intellectual, and a professor who writes and teaches about human rights and combating white supremacy. She describes the call-out culture of public shaming as "toxic" and questions whether it and its cousin, cancel culture, are actually advancing the goals of social justice.

Better, Ross argues, is to "call in," which she defines as "a call out done with love." Calling in, she writes, means correcting those who make mistakes and unwittingly offend privately rather than publicly, or, if publicly, then "with respect." Calling in avoids labels and puritan one-upmanship; it "engages in debates with words and actions of healing and restoration." Ross tells a story of a time in 2017 when she "accidentally misgendered" a student in one of her classes and "froze with shame, expecting to be blasted." Her student, however, put her at ease, saying, "I misgender myself sometimes." Ross concludes her tale by saying: "We need more of this kind of grace."[7]

Finding grace is up to all of us, but we can also be led. I am struck, for instance, by the spread of "Civic Saturdays," a movement begun by Eric Liu and his wife, Jená Cane, the cofounders of Citizen University. Liu is a powerful civic preacher; Civic Saturdays are designed to be the spontaneous churches of civic religion. A service will feature songs, poetry, readings of many different kinds, engagement with one another, and a sermon.[8] Indeed, Liu has published a book titled *Become America: Civic Sermons on Love, Responsibility, and Democracy.*[9] The genius of the Civic Saturdays approach, however, is that the gatherings can happen anywhere a group of people choose to gather, and can be led by anyone who graduates from Liu and Cane's Civic Seminary.

Participants in Civic Saturdays are there to build "fellowship and faith," on the premise that "democracy works only when enough of us believe it works."[10] The assumption is that humans *need* to believe in something bigger than themselves—a source of grace—and that the believing makes that larger thing possible. Equally important, to bring that larger thing about, each of us must believe and commit to changing ourselves.

Spiritual texts often emphasize renewal. Renewals of covenants and vows are a constant theme in the Bible, in both the Old and New Testaments. Renewal and revival of the faith have an equally long history in Islam. Buddhism teaches us to welcome adversity and examine and reflect on our reactions, opening our hearts, awakening our minds, and renewing our connection to the infinity and unity of Buddha nature.

This spiritual element need not be tied to formal religions, however. It can be as simple as a mountain peak, mist on water, a meadow at sunrise. Beauty—particularly natural beauty—renews the soul. It taps the same deep response that faith does, calling to something deep inside and connecting to something larger than ourselves.

Renewal is a posture, a practice, and a philosophy. It requires us to confront, learn, grow, and recommit to our principles with a better understanding of how to achieve them. Would it be better if we got it right the first time? Of course. But we're human. And the risking, falling, reflecting, and trying again pushes us forward. A little grace helps us get there; a larger grace is what we will find when we succeed.

CHAPTER 10

Plures et Unum

What is it with "re" words? Linguist Deborah Fallows tells the story of the Women of the Commons, six women who decided they wanted to do something positive to benefit the sagging community of tiny Eastport, Maine.[1] One of the women, Linda Godfrey, commented on all the "*de*-words" that journalists used in describing Eastport.

The most used *de*-words were words like "depressed," "dependent," "decline," and "despair," and they were usually used in comments about economics, services, schools, and population. It just seemed that the *de*-words were ever-present, even if a story about Eastport was a positive one.

Fallows describes how "the group set forth to crowd out the *de*-words with *re*-words, words like 'rebound,' 'rediscover,' 'redesign,' 'reverse,' 'renew,' 'reenergize,' 'reemerge.'" They pushed reporters and politicians to move from "de" to "re," using the more positive words. The tactic worked, at least in terms of changing the vocabulary of media stories about Eastport. The Women of the Commons concluded that the shift helped the community get unstuck.

Trabian Shorters, a leader of the new America we could and should become, hears those *re*-words very differently. As a former vice president of the Knight Foundation and current CEO of BMe Community, a growing network of African American leaders and innovators, he has developed a powerful approach to social change called "asset-framing," defining people by their aspirations rather than their challenges.[2] But when he describes the kind of transformative leadership America needs in this moment, he distinguishes between "fixers" and "builders."

In any crisis, Shorters says, fixers and builders rush in. "Fixers tend to be problem-focused. They see the devastation. They're the ones who jump up and rush in and make sure that things get stabilized and things are turned around. . . . You can tend to recognize fixers because they'll use words like renew, restore, repeal, replace. They're always trying to get things back to some stability, some sense of predictability that they've been used to."[3]

Builders have a very different mindset. "Builders see that devastation as a blank slate, like whatever the crisis is, whatever is being wiped out, they see it as an opportunity to create something new." Where fixers want to restore an equilibrium, builders are about "unbalancing that equilibrium, trying to find some way forward. The builders tend to use words like create, explore, discover."[4]

For Keith Yamashita, on the other hand, renewal *requires* transformation. Yamashita is an artist-entrepreneur, a deeply creative, intensely focused CEO-whisperer and social change designer who built a Silicon Valley consulting practice over twenty-five years and then had a stroke at age fifty-one.[5] He now teaches and preaches the "trauma-renewal curve," the path from a traumatic experience—illness, loss, failure, cataclysm—through honest self-examination and confrontation to a new and better state.[6]

In his own life, Yamashita explains that in recovering from the stroke, "I had a disruptive realization: A different kind of flourishing might be possible for me on the other side. I could aim for post-traumatic growth."[7] He believes that we can, as individuals, companies, and, I would add, a country, choose renewal and develop the skills to make it happen, over and over again.

Here, then, are three quite different understandings of renewal. I don't think it is accidental that they come from an older affluent white woman, a young Black man, and a gay Asian American middle-aged man. That's the kaleidoscope America is becoming.

It is worth remembering that African Americans, Hispanics, and other groups have had a very specific and negative experience with renewal. James Baldwin said, "urban renewal ought to be called 'Negro removal.'"[8] That was indeed the experience many communities of color had with the sweeping plans in the 1960s to "renew" entire sectors of cities, as it is with gentrification today.

Where renewal is a synonym for "expulsion and exclusion," it is a dangerous euphemism. Yet as we have seen, Baldwin also thought of renewal as "change in the depths." I cannot insist on my definition of the word and the process behind it; I can only offer it once again as a frame for looking backward and forward at the same time, acknowledging pride and shame, coming back to our history again and again as the foundation on which we must now build something new.

When "we the people" came together in 1787 to establish ourselves as a polity under a new Constitution, "we" were white (actually we were propertied white men). The United States has remained a majority-white nation, however "white" is defined.[9]

No more. According to U.S. Census projections in 2018, the nation will become "minority-white" sometime after 2040.[10] Already, whites are no longer a majority of people under eighteen; by 2027, whites will no longer be the majority of all Americans under thirty.[11] 2026, the 250th anniversary of the Declaration of Independence and hence the founding of the country known as the United States of America, will thus be a historical hinge, a transition from 250 years of being a white nation with nonwhite minorities to 250 years—or however long we survive—of something else.

How we Americans define that "something else" is critically important. A frequent descriptor is "majority-minority," meaning that two or more minority groups must come together to create a majority. A better term, I think, is that we will become a plurality nation.

I prefer "plurality" to "majority-minority" because the history of "minorities" in the United States has so often been one of exclusion and oppression. "Plurality," on the other hand, suggests pluralism, an affirmative recognition and valuing of diversity. It also welcomes the possibility of plural identities, reminding us that race or ethnicity, gender, sexual orientation, religion, geography, age, ability or disability, profession, and various other markers of "groupness" can all be different facets of one person. Interestingly, the group of Americans that is projected to grow the most between now and 2060 is "multiracial," albeit from a very small base.[12]

Plurality even holds out the possibility that we could limit what Berkeley law professor john a. powell and his colleague Stephen Menendian identify as our deep human need for "othering" and "belonging."[13] The lines between "us " and "them" so often track lines of division that cannot be chosen, like race, ethnicity, sexual orientation, and disability. Thinking of ourselves as carrying plural identities may make it easier to limit "us" and "them" to more malleable and adoptable affiliations, like fan groups of sports teams or music bands.

———

One way to affirm this new plural identity would be to use the occasion of the 250th anniversary of the founding to change our national motto, "E Pluribus Unum," or "out of many, one," to "Plures et Unum," "many *and* one." Many American conservatives and classical liberals are deeply worried about "multiculturalism," an ideology that, in their view, "seeks to divide and conquer Americans, making many groups out of one citizenry."[14] That same fear powers broader debates over "identity politics," the worry, as scholar and commentator Francis Fukuyama expresses it, that democracies are fracturing into segments based on ever-narrower identities, threatening the possibility of deliberation and collective action by society as a whole.[15]

But why must it be either/or? Why can't we be *plures* and *unum* at the same time? Why can't that very duality be our greatest strength? As Yale psychology professor Jennifer Richeson writes in response to Fukuyama: "Identifying as American does not require the relinquishing of other identities. In fact, it is possible to leverage those identities to cultivate and deepen one's Americanness."[16]

Counterintuitively, it is possible to share experiences of being marginalized, or struggling to find your place in society, in ways that could actually increase social cohesion across very different groups. Tea Party Republicans and Bernie Democrats have experiences in common, as do rural whites and inner-city Blacks. Richeson believes America can have a "unifying national creed that would allow Americans to embrace their own identities, encourage them to respect the identities embraced by others, and affirm shared principles of equality and justice."[17]

Stacey Abrams, the first African American woman to be nominated for governor by a major political party, who came within fifty-four thousand votes of being elected as governor of Georgia, put this view into practice. She "intentionally and vigorously highlighted communities of color and other marginalized groups" during her campaign, "*not to the exclusion of others but as a recognition* of their specific policy needs."[18] After all, she writes, "the marginalized did not create identity politics: their identities have been forced on them by dominant groups."

Like Richeson, Abrams insists that it is possible to embrace "the distinct histories and identities of groups in a democracy" in ways that enhance "the complexity and capacity of the whole." That multiplicity, that pluralism, can be who we are as Americans, in all our glorious and tortured intersections. "By embracing identity and its prickly, uncomfortable contours," Abrams writes, "Americans will become more likely to grow as one."[19]

Best of all, we can borrow from one another. Langston Hughes's "Let America Be America Again" insists that we must renew ourselves to be something we have never yet been. One of his other poems, "Theme for English B," achingly captures the notion of plural identity—identity in the sense of being part of one another:

> I guess being colored doesn't make me not like the same
>   things other folks like who are other races. So will my
>   page be colored that I write?
> Being me, it will not be white. But it will be a part of you,
>   instructor. You are white—yet a part of me, as I am a
>   part of you. That's American. Sometimes perhaps you

don't want to be a part of me. Nor do I often want to
be a part of you. But we are, that's true! As I learn from
you, I guess you learn from me—although you're
older—and white—and somewhat more free.[20]

"That's American." If only it were.

Hughes published "Theme for English B" in 1951. Eighty
years later, his vision is far from achieved. It is interesting to
contrast Hughes with Gregory Pardlo, winner of the Pulitzer
Prize for poetry in 2015 and also an African American man. In
his memoir *Air Traffic*, Pardlo concludes by wanting to "reinvent America. I want to forgive us our history of slavery and the
crackpot invention of race we've used first to maintain that peculiar institution, and then later to designate an exploitable sur-
plus population."

Forgive but not forget. In Pardlo's "new America," Americans
will be constantly reminded of their double-sided history.
"Each July Fourth we will celebrate freedom *and* our ongoing
struggle to defeat selfish and tyrannical impulses in every one
of our American hearts." He imagines a similar duality on all
our holidays: Thanksgiving, Memorial Day, even Columbus
Day, when Americans should remember the *Nina, Pinta*, and
Santa Maria alongside the *Amistad* and other legendary slave
ships, as well as the *Mayflower*.

Pardlo imagines Americans who "revel in the richness of our
diversity" and "celebrate the epic collusion of American culture."[21] *Plures et unum* indeed.

A new American identity and a new American politics needs a
new American patriotism. A way of understanding and

celebrating a love of country that can unite us and move us forward.

As New America staff are all too aware, due to my periodic "Sunday notes," my favorite definition of patriotism comes from Carl Schurz, a German immigrant who served as a Civil War general and later a senator from New York.[22] In remarks to the Senate in 1872, he said: "My country, right or wrong; if right, to be kept right; and if wrong, to be set right."[23] James Baldwin's version of this same sentiment was that he loved America so much that he insisted "on the right to criticize her perpetually."[24]

Patriotism as criticism is an act of accountability and active citizenship, just like voting. Taking a knee during the playing of the national anthem, as quarterback Colin Kaepernick did in 2016 to protest police brutality against African Americans, is a deeply patriotic act. Nonviolent protest, in a system that expects and protects free expression, is a public commitment to setting the country right.

Public criticism of the government—any government—is also an act of faith: the faith that holding authorities and fellow citizens to account for the gap between what they say and what they do will actually matter. Kaepernick and his fellow protesters believe that valuing some American lives less than others because of skin color is un-American and wrong, and that protest within the system can help set it right.

The greatest faith, and thus the greatest love of country, is displayed by those Americans who believe in the country and fight to set it right even when it consistently fails them. Journalist Nikole Hannah-Jones won a Pulitzer Prize for her work on the 1619 Project, an ongoing initiative commemorating four hundred years of African American history in the United States. She began her essay introducing the project with the following line, "My dad always flew an American flag in our front yard."[25]

Hannah-Jones explains that her father had gone into the military but had been treated badly. Growing up, she was embarrassed by his patriotism. Her father's pride "in being an American felt like a marker of his degradation, his acceptance of our subordination." Over time, however, she comes to see his flying of the flag as an act of defiance, an assertion of the indispensable contributions that African Americans have made to building American wealth and power, and of faith. "Our founding ideals were false when they were written," she writes. "Black people have fought to make them true."[26]

Theodore Roosevelt Johnson, a twenty-year Navy veteran, White House Fellow, and author of a book on race, national solidarity, and the future of America, agrees. He sees African Americans as "superlative citizens," practiced at "taking on all the responsibilities required of the citizenry even when the nation does not deliver on its promises."[27] They have also learned to support and stand for one another, he argues, developing the solidarity that the entire nation now needs.

Patriotism as criticism means holding ourselves and our government to account. Patriotism as faith believes that "we," the body politic, mean what we say and will respond to demonstrable hypocrisy. What then, of patriotism as love?

Just as Hannah-Jones describes, people on the left often seem uncomfortable with overt displays of love of country: the flag flying in front of a house or on a lapel pin, the national anthem, the hand on the heart during the Pledge of Allegiance. Perhaps because they are hokey; perhaps because they are too simple to capture a more complicated relationship with one's country. I understand those instincts, but I don't believe we can renew this country without loving it, or at least loving parts of it, and loving one another. I choose to put "Patriot" first on my

Twitter handle to challenge the idea that love and criticism cannot thrive side by side.

━━━━

I love birds. They give me endless amounts of pleasure. As I wrote for *Huffington Post* in 2014, "the moments I spend enjoying them—and yes, talking to them, to my teenage sons' eternal mortification—are moments out of time," suspended in an eternal present.[28] I often say that as long as I am alive enough to enjoy a glass of champagne or a shot of bourbon and watch the birds at my feeder, I want to keep living.

You laugh, perhaps, but birds are beautiful, resourceful, and far smarter than they are given credit for. "Bird brain" should be a compliment.[29] We also now know that birds are the descendants of dinosaurs; watching them is a way of communing with the earth of sixty million years ago. Perhaps someday millions of years in the future, some other species will commune with tiny insect-like hominids, all that is left of us.

Although I never intended to, I have gradually become a passionate amateur birder. When Andy and I travel, I always have my binoculars, asking him frequently to stop so I can get a good look at a bird that I have just spotted, while he mutters under his breath about the purple-spotted yellow-crested flea-flicker. But for me, even a walk around the block is suddenly transformed; I am alert to every note and flash of feathers.

The most important thing I have learned as a birder is that you have to hear before you can see. You have to listen, and then find the source of the sound. Over time, you learn the songs and then the world is forever changed; when I walk on the Delaware-Raritan Canal near my house in Princeton, I can say hello to the catbird and the cardinal and the blue heron, hoping always to hear the shrill, impossibly fast call of the kingfisher. I have woken up to a world I had been only barely aware of.

Waking up to how so many others who are different from me experience the world we supposedly share was a similar experience. For decades I have walked into every meeting or conference or panel and automatically, almost unconsciously, counted how many women were present. A Jewish friend of mine once confided that she automatically counts how many fellow Jews are present. Hana Passen, the young woman whom I hired as my assistant in 2012, who is herself mixed-race and navigates being both Jewish and Black, taught me to count the people of color present.

Counting is never enough. But it is a start. It is the first step toward the awareness that is necessary to build true inclusion. Step two is to wake up to the many subtle slights or put-downs—almost all of them subconscious—in the way the people of color in the room are treated. Again, I do this reflexively when it comes to women; it was not a big leap to see and feel the double burden that women of color so often shoulder and then to extend that awareness to men of color as well.

In the process, however, I came to recognize that for the first two decades of my career, I was much more focused on advancing my own quite specific tribe—white women—than on understanding and appreciating intersectionality, the layered and intersecting disadvantages that women who are also minorities of many different kinds contend with. Today, I am alive to so much more of what is happening around me, even as I strive to deepen my awareness.

Color, of course, is visible, as disabilities, religion, and gender status may be, although only sometimes. So often the differences among us—sexual orientation, class, educational level, political affiliation, and ethnic origin—are hidden or hard to ascertain without careful listening and observation. Yet awareness of and sensitivity to many kinds of difference is necessary for true inclusion.

It is fashionable in many circles—conservative, center-right, but also center-left, at least among some people—to make fun of being "woke." Just how "woke" are you? And how much do you signal "wokeness"? I understand why—the extremes of virtue-signaling drive me crazy, even as I periodically engage in it. But waking up—really waking up to what I am missing in my world has been a critical part of my own renewal.

I say "renewal" here rather than "growth" or "development" because waking up has been the kind of growth that requires *un*learning as much as learning. It requires equal parts humility and confidence—a difficult combination. The humility to challenge your own prior certainties, suspend judgment, and open up to ways of seeing and understanding the world; the confidence to question and disagree, to take risks, and to continue to lead.

Remember the "we" problem? The question of who the "we" is that you are speaking for and who you are *not* speaking for? Cultivated awareness of difference, paradoxically, is part of the path to true inclusion. Extrapolated to the national level, waking up to difference is a way of feeling your own identity in relation to so many other American identities, instead of presuming a common "Americanness." It then becomes all the more imperative to identify and strengthen the identities—as parent or child, brother or sister, worker, fan, volunteer, worshiper, hobbyist, and so many others—that can tie us together.

▬▬

As a white American, a European American, who if I live long enough will spend the last part of my life in an America that is no longer majority white, I think I understand at least some of the fear of the profound demographic and cultural change that many of my fellow white Americans seem to feel. In learning to see our country differently and far more inclusively, I am giving up many of the assumptions, stories, and heroes that I grew up with. I must relinquish the reflexive affirmations that America is an exceptional nation, that we have generally fought on the side of the good and the right, that the horrors of genocide, crimes against humanity, mob justice and massacres, torture and state brutality happened "out there," in the countries that I spent much of my life studying, and not "in here," in my country.

Not completely, of course. I can still find plenty to be proud of, not least the United States' role in World War I and World War II, even if I no longer believe the simple narrative of good versus evil. I can also now put my faith in a new kind of exceptionalism: that my country will be the first democracy to navigate a peaceful and successful transition from a (constructed) racial majority with multiple minorities to a plurality nation. I can embrace a new patriotism, grounded in perpetual renewal.

I can also recognize that while the sense of loss is real, so too is the joy in what I gain. To begin with, I get an entire pantheon of new heroes and a far greater awareness of the cultural and historical richness of my country. Renewing the promise of America can enrich us all.

White Americans have been expecting Americans of every other race, color, and creed to identify with our founding fathers and countless white presidents, generals, inventors, entrepreneurs, and activists for two centuries. Yet if those men should be presumptively celebrated by all Americans, then so too should the men and women dear to other American hearts. When Martin Luther King Jr. Day was established as a federal holiday in 1983, I thought of Dr. King as an African American hero. Today I think of him as an American hero; I thrill to the power and beauty of his words just as I do to the Gettysburg Address.

So bring on heroes and holidays. Any effort at a list is bound to offend, both because of whom it might include and whom it might omit. Yet surely African Americans, Hispanic Americans, Indigenous Americans, Asian Americans, and the many subgroups within these populations can decide on the people they want to venerate. As Gregory Pardlo suggests, we will probably have to double and triple up on existing holidays, remembering many different Americans at the same time. We will also have to learn how to praise and question at the same time, to give up on the idea of pure heroes, and instead see them in the round, as great humans with many flaws.

Harvard political theorist Danielle Allen spent years teaching the Declaration of Independence to a class of adult students in downtown Chicago. She claims the Declaration as her "patrimony," through her African American father and her white Anglo-Saxon Protestant mother, even though neither would have been encompassed by the white men of property our founders sought to secure rights for.[30] Reading it phrase by phrase, she demonstrates to her students and to all of us how the Declaration can bring us together by reconciling the dimensions of the document that often pull us apart.

Allen explains that the Declaration matters "because it helps us see that we cannot have freedom *without* equality."[31] Individuals must be free to be able to come together voluntarily and govern themselves. To stay together, however, enough to defend their collective liberty from either the government or an outside force, they must see and commit to one another as equals.

American political parties have defined themselves in terms of liberty versus equality for generations, albeit under different labels. Conservatives value liberty; progressives value equality. If Allen is right, however, that both are necessary and are indeed preconditions for each other, why not create a party that stands for both liberty *and* equality? Once again, the way forward is both/and.

———

In May 1988, the late, great writer Toni Morrison gave the commencement address at Sarah Lawrence College. "I assume you have been trained to think," she told the graduates, "to have an intelligent encounter with problem-solving." "But I want to talk about the step before that. . . . I want to talk about dreaming."[32]

Talking of dreams may seem highly quixotic in an era in which watching the news is so often the stuff of nightmares. But dreaming is what is going to see us through. "Not idle wishful speculation, but engaged, directed daytime vision," Morrison instructed her audience. "Entrance into another's space, someone else's situation, sphere."[33]

"We are in a mess," she confided. The only way out is the "archaic definition" of "dreaming": "'to envision; a series of images of *unusual vividness, clarity, order and significance.'"[34] Those are precisely the images we need today: vivid, clear, ordered images of what a new America can and will look like, ordered in the pragmatic sequence we will need to bring them about.

Martin Luther King Jr. had a dream that the words of our founders would actually come to pass.[35] Those of us committed to deep change will need to draw on the wells of renewal, to reassure all Americans that room remains for a past that they can be proud of even as we face our shame. We will need to make room for complexity, for holding opposites in our mind at the same time, for faith and forgiveness. But we can dream our way forward. We can not only imagine, but actually *envision* making those dreams real.

CODA

The America That Has Never Been Yet, Yet Must Be

It's 2026. The United States is reflecting on and reckoning with 250 years of history since its founding. It is also celebrating the continuation of our great national experiment, evolving in ways the founders could never imagine.

Villages, towns, and cities across the country, as part of a five-year US@250 project launched in 2021, have been telling their history, their *whole* history. They have worked with the organization Report for America to enlist their young people as local journalists, sending them forth to interview their elders and to dig through crumbling town records of deeds, marriages, births, deaths, and artifacts. They tell stories long buried or never told, discovering the Native American sites the town's ancestors settled on, the many sites of slavery and Jim Crow, the immigrant labor that built their houses and economies, the continual ebb and flow of othering and belonging, exclusion and inclusion, oppression and freedom in the shaping and reshaping of their neighborhoods. Stories of people and events to be celebrated and condemned, of virtue and villainy, heroism and human frailty, individualism and interdependence, risk and resilience, all side by side.

Museums and cultural institutions across the country are holding special exhibits. The Smithsonian is opening the new Museum of the American Latino on the National Mall. Like the Museum of African American History and Culture, it tells the history of Hispanic Americans and their communities; like the National Museum of the American Indian, it celebrates the vibrant presence of Latinx people in contemporary American life. More museums are planned to honor the history, culture, and contributions of different groups of Americans, including European American immigrants from many different countries; the Mall is a big place. The Museum of American History continues to be cherished, however, telling the braided history of one America as honestly as it can.

In 1976, a fleet of sixteen tall ships from around the world sailed into New York harbor. This year, replicas of slave ships are arriving at every port where they once hideously delivered people as cargo, to anchor there as floating museums and memorials. New York is also hosting a fleet of nearly two hundred ships from every country that ever sent an immigrant to the United States, to sail past the Statue of Liberty and Ellis Island before sailing for other ports where immigrants landed on our coasts. Those ports are recognizing and honoring the Native American tribes who once owned the land.

Cities and towns across the country have worked with their sister cities in countries around the world to develop joint ceremonies of celebration or commemoration, emphasizing our deep connections to other nations. They have also invited Native Americans descended from the tribes and nations that once inhabited the land where they sit to design appropriate forms of commemoration.

During the fifteen days between Juneteenth, on June 19, and the Fourth of July, the nation will honor many founders, old and new. In 2021, President Biden put together a National Sestercentennial Commission chaired by former presidents Obama and Bush. The commission's charge was to identify fifty-six additional founders of the United States, to join the fifty-six men in the Second Continental Congress who signed the Declaration of Independence. The inspiration for the commission was Barack Obama's eulogy for congressman and civil rights icon John Lewis, who died in July 2020:

> He as much as anyone in our history brought this country a little bit closer to our highest ideals. And someday, when we do finish that long journey toward freedom; when we do form a more perfect union—whether it's years from now, or decades, or even if it takes another two centuries—John Lewis will be a founding father of that fuller, fairer, better America.[1]

The Fourth of July will also see the signing of the legislation to change our national motto from *E Pluribus Unum* to *Plures et Unum*. The National Truth and Reconciliation Commission, which has been holding hearings and sponsoring many different kinds of events since it was created in 2021, will issue its final report.

The New Frontiers Commission, likewise convened in 2021, will issue a report card on a set of bold national goals to be achieved by 2036: establishing the United States as the world leader in environmental technologies of many different kinds, from reducing carbon emissions to desalination and new reusable materials; pioneering a new generation of both factories and farms tied to local economies; designing new educational systems to ensure that American students rank in the top three countries in all international learning assessments; and creating a health and care system that will address the medical and social determinants of physical and mental health.

Businesses, civic organizations, universities, religious institutions, learned societies, professional associations, local and state governments, and many other groups and institutions are also celebrating the completion of their 2026 Pledges of Allegiance—to America's highest ideals. Over the past five years, beginning in 2021, they have made commitments to achieve specific, measurable goals by 2026.

Many committed to ensure that their people—at every level of leadership and performance—reflected the American population. Many committed to specific equity goals: changes in organizational culture; in their choice of contracting, service, and partner firms and organizations; in the nature of the work they undertake themselves and support in their charitable giving.

Many other organizations and governments committed to accomplishing specific goals in their work by 2026. Here are some of the results.

Twenty-six of the states that are preparing for midterm elections this year will be using some form of ranked-choice voting, with open primaries and nonpartisan redistricting.

Twenty-six states have adopted the Social Progress Index as a measure of their economic and social flourishing, focusing specifically on race, gender, and class disparities.

Twenty-six hundred of the nation's more than thirteen thousand school districts have adopted Community School Acts, allowing individual learners to achieve educational milestones through a combination of school-based and community-based learning.

Ten states have moved to drawing uniform school districts through a bipartisan commission, funding them equally in line with incentives established to receive additional federal funding.

———

So many things have changed. *Fortune* magazine is rolling out its first For-Benefit 500, listing the top public benefit corporations in the country by both market capitalization and social impact, including sustainability, employee development, and community contributions. The Impact Exchange, in which companies are rated as rigorously on a set of impact measures as financial returns, has been up and flourishing for several years.

Worker councils and worker centers have sprung up in businesses and counties across the country, concentrating the power of labor to work with (and, if necessary, against) management to protect the interests of workers. They grew out of worker health councils to protect worker interests during the COVID-19 pandemic.

The Family Security Act, providing every family with a budget for paid family leave to meet whatever care needs may arise, and the Universal Childcare Act have jump-started the core care economy. Millions of jobs have been created and upgraded in the "care plus" or performance economy: counselors, coaches, advisers, mentors, tutors, trainers, navigators, community health and care workers, and many others.

One form of reparations for centuries of slavery, oppression, and discrimination against Black Americans in particular and other communities of color is the new availability of large pools of capital to local entrepreneurs across the country. These funds will be disbursed to everyone, but with a specific focus on people of color and women, particularly women of color, who want to expand or retrofit existing businesses or create new ones.

Many of these new businesses will be connected to the reconstruction and retrofitting of our entire physical infrastructure as part of the Green New Deal, and to building physical, social, and economic resilience in the face of severe weather, drought, floods, and future pandemics. The strip malls of the twentieth century are being torn down, making way in many places for a restoration of native habitat and small farms.

All Americans under eighteen will look forward to their year of National Service, to be completed between the ages of eighteen and twenty-five; older Americans will be able to participate voluntarily.

Finally, we will no longer be debating whether it is the American century or the Chinese century. The United States will be leading the way, through a host of new institutions, to make it the global century, an era in which great power competition takes a back seat to global problem solving.

Many other things have stayed the same, or been mixed and remixed in ways that cast them in a new light. A five-year conversation about national songs and symbols, monuments and rituals, has taken many taboos off the table but has also reaffirmed deep commitments to the anthem, the flag, and other emblems of unity for a plurality nation. On the cultural side, the year kicked off with the opening of Lin-Manuel Miranda's new musical, 2026, on Broadway; within a month it was streaming to theaters across the country. Communities have been holding 2026 parties to watch it together. And composers, rappers, and writers across the country are competing to customize versions of the songs and lyrics for their own hometowns, sparking new conversations about local history.

Painters, poets, composers, musicians, photographers, videographers, filmmakers, quilt-makers, sculptors, virtual reality coders, and artists of many other descriptions have come together in 2026 competitions, expositions, installations, festivals, and virtual events. Two hundred and fifty million Americans, from elementary school students to senior citizens, can point to some way in which they participated in the anniversary, to celebrate, commemorate, re-imagine and renew.

That is one telling of 2026.

What is yours?

What is a dream we have not dared to yet dream, but you want to see be made real?

What will be our new narrative for our country?

Who will be included in the "we, the people"?

What scares you now, but encourages you to run toward a new learning? Confront a bias? Celebrate a legacy?

What will our towns and cities feel like—who will feel seen, heard, honored?

What will your role be in the making of our nation?

And how will you contend with the polarities, and inconsistencies, and hopes, and foibles that make us, us?

If you could find a new strand of possibility with our fellow citizens, what would those strands be?

How would you weave them together?

How would you begin, starting this very moment?

I know how I would end. It's 2026. Throughout the year, the nation's first woman president presides over solemn ceremonies of reckoning, joyful celebrations of renewal, and competitions to imagine what the next fifty or 250 years will bring. In her speeches, she always makes sure to thank her sisters across the land. She thanks them for marching, lobbying, legislating, pushing, problem solving, and acting in every way they could think of. She thanks them for keeping the faith, for believing that change could and would come.

She reflects and represents a new America, a founded and re-founded America with a vision of universal and equal liberty, justice, democracy, prosperity, and security for the next 250 years. She can foresee that the presidential elections of 2028, 2032, 2036, and every four years thereafter will bring a steady progression of "firsts," until all Americans can imagine that they can grow up to be president, or anything else they want to be. Until America is not the country that must be, but the country that is.

ACKNOWLEDGMENTS

So many people to thank! Including many people who deplore my habit of using sentence fragments to introduce paragraphs. I appreciate you even when I ignore your edits.

My deep gratitude goes to my first-round readers, all of you who worked your way through a version that was not yet fully a book. My special thanks to my oldest friend, Janie Battle Richards, and her husband, David Richards, who sat me down on their terrace and explained as nicely as possible that they had found the structure confusing and parts of the draft impenetrable. Keith Yamashita, who has had his own experience of renewal, has been beyond generous, really taking on this project as his own. It is a far better book as a result. Sarah Chayes, a powerful writer and author herself, also proved to be a terrific editor, making suggestions and raising questions that helped me see my own argument more clearly.

Hana Passen and Melody Frierson also read the first draft very carefully and alerted me to many potential pitfalls; their confidence in the project has buoyed my own. As I have written in the text, Cecilia Muñoz and Tyra Mariani were major figures in my own renewal; they were also attentive and supportive readers. New America's board chair Helene Gayle has no time but somehow found enough to read and comment, as did Jeremy Adelman, Christie Henry, Edith Moravcsik, Donna

Norton, Hilary Pennington, Kate Pennington, Bryan Slaughter, Hoke Slaughter, and Alison Yost. I am grateful to you all.

I am also indebted to three anonymous reviewers who took the time to offer detailed and honest comments. Ruth O'Brien first recruited me to write for the Public Square series; her enthusiasm for the project at every stage was infectious and appreciated.

My second-round readers got me over the finish line by pushing me to revise one more time. Gordon LaForge and Sara Blues came in at just the right moment and suggested a new structure. Hilary Cottam, Allison Stanger, Olivia Albrecht, and Melody Frierson, again, all made valuable comments. Bob and Nan Keohane challenged me with the love and honesty that close friendship allows.

Others read only parts of the manuscript but lent their perspectives and expertise. I thank Roy Bahat, Elana Berkowitz, Alan Davidson, Lee Drutman, Michael Feigelson, Sara Fenske, Lisa Kelley, Rachel Levin, Courtney Leimkuhler, Martha Metz, Gemma Mortensen, and Matthew Stepka. Some of the chapters you read did not make it into the final draft, but your work was not in vain, as I hope to show in future writing.

A different kind of thanks goes to my extraordinary colleagues on the core team for the US@250 project. Over a year of meetings, you have sharpened my sensibilities and deepened my understanding of the deep humanity and justice it will take to build an America "big enough to hold us all."

I could not have written the book without the tremendous research assistance and citation support provided by Kazumi Hoshino-Macdonald. They will be writing their own books before long! Denise Barksdale ferociously protected my time to make it possible for me to revise and provided unwavering moral support. Terry Murphy has been with me through every book I've written; I value her comments, her judgment, and her remarkable ability to do whatever needs doing.

Princeton University Press has been a pleasure to work with. My editor, Eric Crahan, deftly shepherded the book through its various incarnations. Madeleine Adams is a superb copyeditor, with a light but unerring touch. I am also grateful for the entire production and publicity team: Danielle Amatucci, Will Brown, Kate Farquhar-Thomson, Thalia Leaf, Terri O'Prey, Laurie Schlesinger, Karl Spurzem, and Maria Whelan. Laura Vignale also provided an extra boost on the cover design.

An agent is part salesperson, negotiator, and therapist. Will Lippincott of Aevitas excels at all three; I couldn't write a book without him.

Finally, as always, I thank my sons, Edward and Alexander, for their absolute belief that "of course you can do it!" and the joy and love they bring to my life. And to my husband, Andy, who is often my toughest critic but always my most constant supporter. You make me laugh every day.

NOTES

Preface

1. Anne-Marie Slaughter, "Why Women Still Can't Have It All," *The Atlantic*, July/August 2012, https://www.theatlantic.com/magazine/archive/2012/07/why-women-still-cant-have-it-all/309020/.

2. For an illustration of this critique, see Ashley Fetters, "4 Big Problems with *The Feminine Mystique*," *The Atlantic*, February 12, 2013, https://www.theatlantic.com/sexes/archive/2013/02/4-big-problems-with-the-feminine-mystique/273069/.

Introduction: When Leadership Means Having to Say You're Sorry

1. Frederick Douglass, "What to the Slave Is the Fourth of July?" speech delivered in Rochester, New York, July 5, 1852, reprinted in *The Frederick Douglass Papers*, John W. Blassingame and Peter P. Hinks, eds., Series One, vol. 2 (New Haven, CT: Yale University Press, 2003).

2. B. Drummond Ayres Jr., "Thomas Jefferson's Descendants Continue to Serve," *New York Times*, July 5, 1976, https://www.nytimes.com/1976/07/05/archives/thomas-jeffersons-descendants-continue-to-serve.html.

3. Annette Gordon-Reed, *Thomas Jefferson and Sally Hemings: An American Controversy* (Charlottesville: University of Virginia Press, 1998).

4. "Thomas Jefferson and Sally Hemings: A Brief Account," Monticello, accessed July 29, 2020, https://www.monticello.org/thomas-jefferson/jefferson-slavery/thomas-jefferson-and-sally-hemings-a-brief-account/.

5. Lin-Manuel Miranda, "Cabinet Battle #1," from *Hamilton*, 2015.

6. Hannah Knowles, "As Plantations Talk More Honestly about Slavery, Some Visitors Are Pushing Back," *Washington Post*, September 8, 2019, https://www.washingtonpost.com/history/2019/09/08/plantations-are-talking-more-about-slavery-grappling-with-visitors-who-talk-back/.

7. "Renewal," Merriam-Webster's Learner's Dictionary, accessed January 8, 2021, https://www.learnersdictionary.com/definition/renewal.

8. My friend Rachel Levin drew my attention to a quotation from meditation teacher and author Sharon Salzberg that captures this idea brilliantly. "If you have to let go of distractions and begin again, thousands of times, fine. That's not a roadblock to the practice—that is the practice. That's life: starting over, one breath at a time." Sharon Salzberg, *Real Happiness, 10th Anniversary Edition: A 28-Day Program to Realize the Power of Meditation*, 2nd ed. (New York: Workman, 2019), 51–52.

9. The full quotation from Baldwin is: "It is the responsibility of free men to trust and to celebrate what is constant—birth, struggle, and death are constant, and so is love, thought we may not always think so—and to apprehend the nature of change, to be able and willing to change. I speak of change not on the surface but in the depths—change in the sense of renewal. But renewal becomes impossible if one supposes things to be constant that are not—safety, for example, or money, or power. One clings then to chimeras, by which one can only be betrayed, and the entire hope—the entire possibility—of freedom disappears." James Baldwin, *The Fire Next Time* (New York: Vintage International, 1993), 91–92.

10. For a description of towns and small cities renewing their physical architecture this way across the country, see James Fallows and Deborah Fallows, *Our Towns: A 100,000 Journey into the Heart of America*, reprint ed. (New York: Vintage, 2019).

11. John Gardner, "Personal Renewal," speech delivered at McKinsey & Company, Phoenix, AZ, November 10, 1990, https://www.pbs.org/johngardner/sections/writings_speech_1.html.

12. John W. Gardner, *Self-Renewal: The Individual and the Innovative Society*, reprint ed. (Brattleboro, VT: Echo Point Books & Media, 2015), 8.

13. Gardner, *Self-Renewal*, 1.

14. Isabelle Wilkerson, *Caste: The Origins of Our Discontents* (New York: Random House, 2020), 43.

15. Soraya Nadia McDonald, "The Dangerous Magical Thinking of 'This Is Not Who We Are,'" *The Undefeated*, January 14, 2021, https://theundefeated.com/features/capitol-attack-trump-the-dangerous-magical-thinking-of-this-is-not-who-we-are/.

16. Omar El Akkad, *American War: A Novel* (New York: Knopf, 2017).

17. See Gail Collins, *No Stopping Us Now: The Adventures of Older Women in American History* (Boston: Little, Brown, 2019); and Rebecca Traister, *Good and Mad: The Revolutionary Power of Women's Anger* (New York: Simon and Schuster, 2018).

18. Traister, *Good and Mad*.

19. Brittney Cooper, *Eloquent Rage: A Black Feminist Discovers Her Superpower* (New York: St. Martin's Press, 2018). See also Soraya Chemaly, *Rage Becomes Her: The Power of Women's Anger* (New York: Atria Books, 2018).

20. Ruby Sales, "Where Does It Hurt?," *On Being with Krista Tippett*, podcast, https://onbeing.org/programs/ruby-sales-where-does-it-hurt/, quoted in Brian Stout, "The Anger of Hope vs the Anger of Despair," *Building Belonging*, December 9, 2019, https://citizenstout.substack.com/p/the-anger-of-hope-vs-the-anger-of.

21. The Combahee River Collective, "The Combahee River Collective Statement," in *Capitalist Patriarchy and the Case for Socialist Feminism*, ed. Zillah R. Eisenstein (New York: Monthly Review Press, 1977); Kimberle Crenshaw, "Demarginalizing the Intersection of Race and Sex: A Black Feminist Critique of Antidiscrimination Doctrine, Feminist Theory and Antiracist Politics," *University of Chicago Legal Forum* 1989, no. 1 (December 7, 2015), https://chicagounbound.uchicago.edu/uclf/vol1989/iss1/8.

Chapter 1: Run toward the Criticism

1. David Bradford and Carole Robin, *Connect: Building Exceptional Relationships with Family, Friends, and Colleagues* (New York: Currency, 2021), 141.

2. Alice H. Eagly and Sabine Sczesny, "Editorial: Gender Roles in the Future? Theoretical Foundations and Future Research Directions," *Frontiers in Psychology* (September 4, 2019), https://doi.org/10.3389/fpsyg.2019.01965.

3. Katty Kay and Claire Shipman, *The Confidence Code: The Science and Art of Self-Assurance—What Women Should Know* (New York: Harper Business, 2014).

4. Michelle Obama, *Becoming* (New York: Crown Publishing, 2018), 205–6.

5. Cecilia Muñoz, *More than Ready* (New York: Seal Press, 2020).

6. Brené Brown, *Daring Greatly: How the Courage to Be Vulnerable Transforms the Way We Live, Love, Parent, and Lead* (New York: Avery, 2015).

7. Darnell L. Moore, *No Ashes in the Fire: Coming of Age Black and Free in America* (New York: Bold Type Books, 2019), 179. Moore writes about how much he has come to "value the practice of critical self-reflection. It is the internal practice that has catalyzed internal transformation throughout my life and has made it possible for me to minimize the ways I harmed people I have built relationships and communities with." He then applies this lens to the Movement for Black Lives, arguing that anyone "who claims to be part of this work" must themselves engage in critical self-reflection to "assess the extent to which our ideas and practices suffocate some black people." He is outlining a practice of radical honesty not as a license for endless introspection but as an engine for change.

8. Moore, *No Ashes in the Fire*, 11.

9. Moore tells a story of growing up poor, Black, and gay in Camden, New Jersey, and his complicated struggles with his family, his church, and the many layers of his identity. His is ultimately a journey of self-discovery, healing, critical self-reflection, and "black radical love and justice" (*No Ashes in the Fire*, 189). Kiese Laymon's *Heavy: An American Memoir* (New York: Scribner, 2018) is written as a book-length letter to his mother, with emotion so raw that it almost tears the page. He ends by connecting his own healing with the healing of the nation. Gregory Pardlo is a Pulitzer Prize–winning poet. His memoir is titled *Air Traffic: A Memoir of Ambition and Manhood in America* (New York: Knopf, 2018), a reference to his father's firing by Ronald Reagan, alongside thirteen thousand other federal air traffic controllers, to break their strike

in 1981. Pardlo recounts the trail of destruction left in the wake of the firing: the loss of self-esteem, the collapse of a marriage, the spiraling downward out of the middle class. His exploration of his relationship with his father is unflinchingly honest, as is his assessment of himself. He too concludes with a new vision of America. Other memoirs in this same vein of honest introspection mixed with social reflection and critique from women include Natasha Trethewey, *Memorial Drive: A Daughter's Memoir* (New York: Harper Collins, 2020); Julie Lythcott-Haims, *Real American: A Memoir* (New York: Henry Holt, 2017); and Aarti Namdev Shahani, *Here We Are: American Dreams, American Nightmare* (New York: Celadon Books, 2019).

10. Laymon, *Heavy*, 230.

11. The National Memorial for Peace and Justice, https://museumandmemorial .eji.org/memorial.

12. Amanda Ripley, "Complicating the Narratives," blog post, June 27, 2018, updated January 11, 2019, https://thewholestory.solutionsjournalism.org/complicating -the-narratives-b91ea06ddf63. See also Amanda Ripley, *High Conflict: Why We Get Trapped and How We Get Out* (New York: Simon and Schuster, 2021).

13. Peter Coleman, *The Five Percent: Finding Solutions to Seemingly Impossible Conflicts* (New York: Public Affairs, 2011).

14. Ripley, "Complicating the Narratives."

15. Ripley, "Complicating the Narratives."

16. Homer, *The Odyssey*, trans. Emily Wilson (New York: W. W. Norton, 2017).

17. Homer, *The Odyssey*, trans. Robert Fagles (New York: Penguin Classics, 1999).

18. I also read Daniel Mendelsohn's book *An Odyssey: A Father, a Son, and an Epic* (New York: Knopf, 2017), about his odyssey with his own father. Mendelsohn himself is a classics professor at Bard College; he teaches a course on *The Odyssey* that his father chooses to audit; the two of them later take an Odyssey cruise in the Mediterranean designed to retrace Odysseus's voyage. It's a complicated but compelling intertwining of the timeless themes of Odysseus's journey with the narrative of his own life, one that made me reflect on mine.

19. Homer, *The Odyssey* (1999), 61.

20. Homer, *The Odyssey* (2017), 9.

21. Homer, *The Odyssey* (2017), 524.

22. See Madeline Miller, *Circe* (Little, Brown and Company, 2018); Pat Barker, *The Silence of the Girls* (New York: Knopf Doubleday, 2018).

23. Homer, *The Odyssey* (2017), 432.

Chapter 2: Connect to Change

1. Winston Churchill, "Never Give In, Never, Never, Never," speech delivered at Harrow School, October 29, 1941, https://www.nationalchurchillmuseum.org/never-give -in-never-never-never.html. Original statement is "Never give in, never, never, never. . . ."

2. Hillary Clinton, "'Resist, Insist, Persist, Enlist': Hillary Clinton Speech Targets Trump," CBS News, March 28, 2017, https://www.cbsnews.com/news/resist-insist -persist-enlist-hillary-clinton-speech-targets-trump/.

3. Ama Marston and Stephanie Marston, *Type R: Transformative Resilience for Thriving in a Turbulent World* (New York: Public Affairs, 2018). I had also read and been inspired by Andrew Zolli and Ann Marie Healy's book, *Resilience: Why Things Bounce Back* (New York: Free Press, 2012), which offers a similarly dynamic concept of resilience in a "world that is intrinsically out of order." Andrew Zolli, "A Shift to Humility: Resilience and Expanding the Edge of Change," podcast, *On Being with Krista Tippett*, May 15, 2013, https://onbeing.org/programs/andrew-zolli-a-shift-to -humility-resilience-and-expanding-the-edge-of-change/.

4. Marston and Marston, *Type R*, 19–20.

5. Angela Duckworth, *Grit: The Power of Passion and Perseverance* (New York: Scribner, 2016).

6. Anne-Marie Slaughter, *The Chessboard and the Web: Strategies of Connection in a Networked World* (New Haven, CT: Yale University Press, 2017).

7. Joshua A. Geltzer, "Building Resilience on Modern Communications Platforms," in *Resilience* (Washington, DC: New America, 2020), https://resilience .newamerica.org/building-resilience-on-modern-communications-platforms/.

8. Yuval Noah Harari, *Sapiens: A Brief History of Humankind* (New York: Harper Perennial, 2018), 41.

9. Cecilia Muñoz, "The Bigger Burden Is Pretending You're Not Scared," in *Resilience* (Washington, DC: New America, 2020), https://resilience.newamerica.org /the-bigger-burden/.

10. Marcia Chatelain, "Grit and the College Campus," in *Resilience* (Washington, DC: New America, 2020), https://resilience.newamerica.org/grit-and-the-college -campus/.

11. Chatelain, "Grit and the College Campus."

12. Dr. Louise Aaronson offers an interesting parallel in examining her own medical profession. She finds that medical leaders focus far too much on individual responses to what has become an epidemic of physician burnout and far too little on the systemic and structural causes. Louise Aronson, *Elderhood: Redefining Aging, Transforming Medicine, Reimagining Life* (New York: Bloomsbury, 2019).

13. Walmart, "America at Work: A National Mosaic and Roadmap for Tomorrow," 2019, https://corporate.walmart.com/media-library/document/america-at-work -report/_proxyDocument?id=00000168-dec5-d9f9-a7f8-deed73c70001.

14. Walmart, "America at Work."

15. Sean Safford, *Why the Garden Club Couldn't Save Youngstown: The Transformation of the Rust Belt* (Cambridge, MA: Harvard University Press, 2009).

16. Robert Putnam, *Bowling Alone: The Collapse and Revival of American Community* (New York: Simon and Schuster, 2001), 19.

17. https://www.thread.org/.

18. https://www.aspeninstitute.org/programs/weave-the-social-fabric-initiative/.

19. Atul Gawande, *Being Mortal: Medicine and What Matters in the End* (New York: Henry Holt, 2014), 248.

20. Milton Mayeroff, *On Caring* (New York: Harper & Row, 1971).

21. Mayeroff, *On Caring,* 7.

Chapter 3: Rethink Risk

1. In addition to the sources cited in this chapter, I owe this insight to my friend David Richards, an entrepreneur who made this point to me very directly after reading a draft of this book. See also Adam Grant, *Originals: How Non-Conformists Move the World* (New York: Penguin Books, 2017), 17, pointing out that successful entrepreneurs were more likely to keep their day jobs while experimenting with something new, hedging their bets.

2. Mariana Mazzucato, *The Entrepreneurial State: Debunking Public vs. Private Sector Myths* (London: Anthem Press, 2013).

3. Formerly, the Woodrow Wilson School of Public and International Affairs at Princeton University.

4. Eric Schmidt and Jonathan Rosenberg, *How Google Works* (New York: Grand Central Publishing, 2014).

5. Cordelia Fine, *Testosterone Rex: Myths of Sex, Science, and Society* (New York: W. W. Norton, 2017), 26.

6. Another factor in a woman's assessment of the risk she faces is that women's mistakes are judged more harshly than men's because "information that supports pre-existing stereotypes tends to be noticed and remembered." See Joan Williams and Rachel Dempsey, *What Works for Women at Work: Four Patterns Working Women Need to Know* (New York: NYU Press, 2016), 25. In other words, if a male boss has doubts about whether the woman employee is a good fit to begin with, her mistake will confirm that stereotype, whereas if a man makes the same mistake, the reaction is more likely to be "everyone makes mistakes."

7. John Coates, *The Hour between Dog and Wolf: Risk-Taking, Gut Feelings and the Biology of Boom and Bust* (New York: Penguin Press, 2012), 273–74.

8. Christine R. Harris, Michael Jenkins, and Dale Glaser, "Gender Differences in Risk Assessment: Why Do Women Take Fewer Risks than Men?," *Judgment and Decision Making* 1, no. 1 (2006): 48–63.

9. Grant, *Originals,* 7.

10. Michelle Gelfand, *Rule Makers, Rule Breakers: Tight and Loose Cultures and the Secret Signals That Direct Our Lives* (New York: Scribner, 2018).

11. Laymon, *Heavy,* 182–83.

12. Rita G. McGrath, "Failing by Design," *Harvard Business Review*, April 2011, https://hbr.org/2011/04/failing-by-design.

13. Mazzucato, *The Entrepreneurial State.*

14. Sam Altman, "Affordable Care," blog post, January 13, 2017, https://blog.samaltman.com/affordable-care.

15. Americans for the Arts, "Statement on Arts and The Affordable Care Act," Arts Mobilization Center, 2017, https://www.americansforthearts.org/news-room/arts-mobilization-center/statement-on-arts-and-the-affordable-care-act.

16. Soo Youn, "40% of Americans Don't Have $400 in the Bank for Emergency Expenses: Federal Reserve," ABC News, May 24, 2019, https://abcnews.go.com/US/10-americans-struggle-cover-400-emergency-expense-federal/story?

17. Libby Reder, Shelly Steward, and Natalie Foster, "Designing Portable Benefits: A Resource Guide for Policymakers," The Aspen Institute—Future of Work Initiative, June 2019, https://assets.aspeninstitute.org/content/uploads/2019/06/Designing-Portable-Benefits_June-2019_Aspen-Institute-Future-of-Work-Initiative.pdf.

18. Lionel Trilling, *Sincerity and Authenticity* (Cambridge, MA: Harvard University Press, 1971).

19. Brené Brown, *Daring Greatly.*

20. Trethewey, *Memorial Drive*, 17.

Chapter 4: Lead from the Center and the Edge

1. Nannerl O. Keohane, *Thinking about Leadership* (Princeton, NJ: Princeton University Press, 2012), 23.

2. Carol Gilligan, *In a Different Voice: Psychological Theory and Women's Development* (Cambridge, MA: Harvard University Press, 1982).

3. https://www.hup.harvard.edu/catalog.php?isbn=9780674970960.

4. Gilligan, *In a Different Voice*, 62.

5. Slaughter, *The Chessboard and the Web*, chapter 8.

6. Anne-Marie Slaughter, "America's Edge: Power in the Networked Century," *Foreign Affairs*, January/February 2009, https://www.foreignaffairs.com/articles/united-states/2009-01-01/americas-edge.

7. Jonathan Haidt, *The Righteous Mind: Why Good People Are Divided by Politics and Religion* (New York: Vintage, 2013).

8. Mary P. Follett, *Dynamic Administration: The Collected Papers of Mary Parker Follett*, ed. E. M. Fox and L. Urwick (London: Pitman, 1940).

9. I am deeply grateful to Keith Yamashita for helping me crystallize this insight.

10. Tressie McMillan Cottom, *Thick: And Other Essays* (New York: New Press, 2019), 195–223. Cottom has a bitingly funny essay titled "Girl 6," in which she

canvasses a number of prominent white male newspaper columnists and discovers that each of them follows only six Black women out of the several hundred people they follow on Twitter.

11. Shoshana Zuboff, "The Coup We Are Not Talking About," *New York Times*, January 29, 2021, https://www.nytimes.com/2021/01/29/opinion/sunday/facebook -surveillance-society-technology.html.

12. The Combahee River Collective, "The Combahee River Collective Statement."

13. Cooper, *Eloquent Rage*, 172.

14. Cottom, *Thick*, 40.

15. John S. Ahlquist and Margaret Levi, *In the Interest of Others: Organizations and Social Activism* (Princeton, NJ: Princeton University Press, 2014).

Chapter 5: Share Power

1. Here I am once again indebted to John Gardner, who notes: "While children quickly learn about the impact that others have on them, even adults well into middle age are slow to understand the impact they have on others." Gardner, "Personal Renewal."

2. When I was a law professor, one of my favorite articles that helped explain both how the law works and ultimately why it works was "The Giving Reasons Requirement," by a deeply learned, wry, and wonderful scholar from Berkeley named Martin Shapiro. Shapiro was a comparative lawyer, someone who studied legal systems in different countries around the world and thought hard about what they had in common. He pointed out that at the core of the rule of law is the idea that the government must give reasons for what it does. "Giving reason requirements are not giving reasons to judges . . . but giving reasons to the public. . . . Administrators must inform citizens of what they are doing and why. Such requirements are a mild self-enforcing mechanism for controlling discretion." See Martin Shapiro, "The Giving Reasons Requirement," *University of Chicago Legal Forum*, no. 1 (1992): 179–220, http:// chicagounbound.uchicago.edu/uclf/vol1992/iss1/8?utm_source=chicagounbound .uchicago.edu%2Fuclf%2Fvol1992%2Fiss1%2F8&utm_medium=PDF&utm _campaign=PDFCoverPages.

3. David Kushner, "Facebook Philosophy: Move Fast and Break Things," *IEEE Spectrum*, June 1, 2011, https://spectrum.ieee.org/at-work/innovation/facebook -philosophy-move-fast-and-break-things.

4. Stanley McChrystal et al., *Team of Teams: New Rules of Engagement for a Complex World* (New York: Portfolio, 2015).

5. Rosalind Adams, "They Used to Be Strangers. Now They're Organizing Some of the Largest Protests In America's Biggest City," *BuzzFeed*, June 16, 2020,

https://www.buzzfeednews.com/article/rosalindadams/the-black-lives-matter -protests-no-central-leadership; Ashley Cole, "Black Lives Matter: Decentralised Leadership and the Problems of Online Organising," *The Conversation*, 2020, https:// theconversation.com/black-lives-matter-decentralised-leadership-and-the -problems-of-online-organising-140897. The Movement for Black Lives describes the Movement as "an ecosystem of individuals and organizations creating a shared vision and policy agenda to win rights, recognition, and resources for Black people." See https://m4bl.org/black-power-rising/.

6. For an overview of the role of technology in catalyzing horizontal movements, see Gideon Rachman et al., "Leaderless Rebellion: How Social Media Enables Global Protests," *Financial Times*, 2019, https://www.ft.com/content/19dc5dfe-f67b -11e9-a79c-bc9acae3b654; and Samuel Brannen, "The Age of Leaderless Revolution," CSIS, November 1, 2019, https://www.csis.org/analysis/age-leaderless -revolution.

7. Peter Senge, Hal Hamilton, and John Kania, "The Dawn of System Leadership," *Stanford Social Innovation Review*, Winter 2015, https://ssir.org/articles/entry/the _dawn_of_system_leadership.

8. Senge, Hamilton, and Kania, "The Dawn of System Leadership."

9. See Tara Dawson McGuinness and Hana Schank, *Power to the Public: The Promise of Public Interest Technology* (Princeton, NJ: Princeton University Press, 2021).

Chapter 6: Looking Backward and Forward

1. Gardner, "Personal Renewal," https://www.pbs.org/johngardner/sections /writings_speech_1.html.

2. For a discussion of how many Black Americans hear the frequent assertion "this is not who we are" by white Americans in the face of violence and overt racism, see Soraya Nadia McDonald, "The Dangerous Magical Thinking of 'This Is Not Who We Are,'" *The Undefeated*, January 14, 2021, https://theundefeated.com /features/capitol-attack-trump-the-dangerous-magical-thinking-of-this-is-not-who -we-are/.

3. Anne-Marie Slaughter, *The Idea That Is America: Keeping Faith with Our Values in a Dangerous World* (New York: Basic Books, 2007).

4. Martin Luther King Jr., "I Have a Dream," speech given at the March on Washington for Jobs and Freedom, Washington, DC, August 28, 1963, https://www .americanrhetoric.com/speeches/mlkihaveadream.htm. Even the idea of "white" men, which was on the books of many states by the time Jefferson wrote the Declaration of Independence, was constructed to differentiate and subjugate nonwhite men. See Nell Irvin Painter, *The History of White People* (New York: W. W. Norton, 2011).

5. Amanda Gorman, "The Hill We Climb," https://www.cnn.com/2021/01/20/politics/amanda-gorman-inaugural-poem-transcript/index.html.

Chapter 7: Rugged Interdependence

1. Cokie Roberts, *Founding Mothers: The Women Who Raised Our Nation* (New York: Harper Perennial, 2005).

2. Many white Americans were deeply dependent on enslaved African Americans, including many white women who actively participated in the economic and social structures of slavery. See Stephanie E. Jones-Rogers, *They Were Her Property: White Women as Slave Owners in the American South* (New Haven, CT: Yale University Press, 2019).

3. For an overview of the goals of the kind of women's history that Davis pioneered, see Natalie Zemon Davis, "'Women's History' in Transition: The European Case," *Feminist Studies* 3, no. 3/4 (1976): 83–103, https://doi.org/10.2307/3177729.

4. Howard Zinn, *A People's History of the United States* (New York: Harper Perennial Modern Classics, 1980).

5. For new attempts at reconstructing American history through diverse lenses, see Penguin Random House's Revisioning History series. These books catalogue the underrepresented origins of indigenous, queer, Latinx, and African American peoples in crafting the United States we know today. See also Jill Lepore, *These Truths: A History of the United States* (New York: W. W. Norton, 2018), where she documents the story of women and people of color in crafting America's political culture. Lepore gathers as many accounts of different peoples as possible into one flowing narrative of U.S. history. It is a seemingly impossible task even for ten or a hundred volumes, but Lepore's is a history in which many Americans can at least begin to see the traces of their ancestors.

6. See Nell Irvin Painter, *Southern History across the Color Line* (Chapel Hill: University of North Carolina Press, 2002); Nell Irvin Painter, *Sojourner Truth: A Life, a Symbol* (New York: W. W. Norton, 1997); and Nell Irvin Painter, *The History of White People* (New York: W. W. Norton, 2011).

7. Alexis de Tocqueville, *Democracy in America* (Chicago: University of Chicago Press, 2006), 3.

8. Tocqueville, *Democracy in America*, 180.

9. Philip Babcock Gove, ed., *Webster's Third New International Dictionary, Unabridged* (Springfield, MA: Merriam-Webster, 1993).

10. Lidian Emerson, "Transcendental Bible," in *The American Transcendentalists: Essential Writings*, ed. Lawrence Buell (New York: Modern Library Classics, 2006), 177.

11. Ralph Waldo Emerson, "Self-Reliance," in *The American Transcendentalists*, 211, 228, 231, 223.

12. Lidian Emerson, "Transcendental Bible," 175.

13. Ralph Waldo Emerson, "Self-Reliance," 219.

14. Ralph Waldo Emerson, "Self-Reliance," 219.

15. Margaret Fuller, "Recollection of Mystical Experiences," in *The American Transcendentalists*, 159–60.

16. George Ripley et al., "Brook Farm's Constitution of 1884," in *The American Transcendentalists*, 239; Ralph Waldo Emerson, "The Significance of British West Indian Emancipation," in *The American Transcendentalists*, 352.

17. Henry David Thoreau, "Walking," *The Atlantic*, June 1862, https://www.theatlantic.com/magazine/archive/1862/06/walking/304674/.

18. Patricia Molen Van Ee, "Women on the Move: Overland Journeys to California," Library of Congress, December 2001, https://guides.loc.gov/american-women-essays/overland-journeys-to-california.

19. Frank McLynn, *Wagons West: The Epic Story of America's Overland Trails*, 1st ed. (New York: Grove Press, 2002), 233.

20. Martha L. Smith, "Going to God's Country," in *A Treasury of American Folklore: Stories, Ballads, and Traditions of the People*, ed. Benjamin A. Botkin, with a foreword by Carl Sandburg (New York: Crown, 1944; reissued, Guilford, CT: Globe Pequot, 2016), 302.

21. Erik Larson, *The Devil in the White City: Murder, Magic, and Madness at the Fair That Changed America* (New York: Vintage, 2004), 5.

22. "A Voice for Justice: The Life and Legacy of Ida B. Wells," University of Chicago Library, https://www.lib.uchicago.edu/collex/exhibits/voice-for-justice-life-and-legacy-ida-b-wells/worlds-columbian-exposition/.

23. Frederick Jackson Turner, "The Significance of the Frontier in American History," 1893, American Historical Association, https://www.historians.org/about-aha-and-membership/aha-history-and-archives/historical-archives/the-significance-of-the-frontier-in-american-history-(1893).

24. More precisely, the American frontier is the place where the complex conditions of civilized European life meet the primitive conditions of preindustrial society over and over again. In the first stage, the "wilderness masters the colonist." But then in the second and third stages, the colonist—whether trader, rancher, farmer, or miner (there were many frontiers)—gradually reestablishes civilization, but with a distinctively American twist.

25. Turner, "The Significance of the Frontier in American History."

26. Turner, "The Significance of the Frontier in American History."

27. Kenneth L. Holmes, *Covered Wagon Women: Diaries and Letters from the Western Trains, 1840–1849*, vol. 1 (Lincoln: University of Nebraska Press, 1983).

28. Political scientist Ruth O'Brien captures this enduring image perfectly in her analysis of how Barack Obama thinks about the role of the state. "Rather than having

the state regulate society, or having society free from state regulation," Obama sees a collaboration between state and market, a society in which individuals come together to forge alliances and create "collective goodwill." This "third tradition," O'Brien continues, "is not the cowboy image" of a life with no constraints, alone on the range. Nor is it an image of "a nursemaid or nanny state" helping people while dictating the details of their lives. It is the image of "pioneers depending on one another in a wagon train—in a collectivity." See Ruth O'Brien, *Out of Many, One: Obama and the Third American Political Tradition* (Chicago: University of Chicago Press, 2013), xv, 3.

29. Louise W. Knight, *Citizen: Jane Addams and the Struggle for Democracy* (Chicago: University of Chicago Press, 2005), 83.

30. Knight, *Citizen*, 181.

31. As Addams wrote, "Hull-House was soberly opened on the theory that the dependence of classes on each other is reciprocal; and that as the social relation is essentially a reciprocal relation, it gives a form of expression that has peculiar value." Jane Addams, *Twenty Years at Hull-House* (New York: Macmillan, 1910), 91.

32. Herbert Hoover, *American Individualism* (Garden City, NY: Doubleday, Page, 1922). At the time, Hoover was serving as secretary of commerce in the Harding administration.

33. Hoover, Campaign speech, "Principles and Ideals of the United States Government," October 22, 1928, Presidential Speeches, https://millercenter.org/the-presidency/presidential-speeches/october-22-1928-principles-and-ideals-united-states-government. Based on the demography of the Midwest in the nineteenth century, it is fair to say that he was thinking about Anglo-Saxon, German, and Nordic men.

34. Hoover, *American Individualism*, 10.

35. Franklin D. Roosevelt, "Commonwealth Club Address," September 23, 1932, https://teachingamericanhistory.org/library/document/commonwealth-club-address/.

36. Hoover, Campaign Speech, 1928.

37. King, "I Have a Dream" speech, https://www.americanrhetoric.com/speeches/mlkihaveadream.htm.

38. Martin Luther King Jr., "Letter from a Birmingham Jail" (Birmingham, AL, 1963), https://kinginstitute.stanford.edu/king-papers/documents/letter-birmingham-jail.

39. Colson Whitehead, *The Underground Railroad* (New York: Penguin Random House, 2016), 272.

40. Botkin, *A Treasury of American Folklore*.

41. David A. Hollinger and Charles Capper, *The American Intellectual Edition* (New York: Oxford University Press, 2011).

42. Muñoz, *More than Ready*, 8.

43. James McWilliams, "Bryan Stevenson on What Well-Meaning White People Need to Know about Race," *Pacific Standard*, February 6, 2019, https://psmag.com/magazine/bryan-stevenson-ps-interview.

44. See Jon Meacham, *The Soul of America: The Battle for Our Better Angels* (New York: Random House, 2018).

Chapter 8: Building Big

1. Andrew McAfee and Eric Brynjolfsson, *The Second Machine Age: Work, Progress, and Prosperity in a Time of Brilliant Technologies* (New York: W. W. Norton, 2014).

2. Lawrence Buell, "Introduction," in *The American Transcendentalists: Essential Writings*, ed. Lawrence Buell (New York: Modern Library Classics, 2006), xxv.

3. See, e.g., David Robertson, with Kent Lineback, *The Power of Little Ideas: A Low-Risk, High-Reward Approach to Innovation* (Boston: Harvard Business School Press, 2017); Owain Service and Rory Gallagher, *Think Small: The Surprisingly Simple Ways to Reach Big Goals* (London: Michael Omara, 2017).

4. Edison is supposed to have made this remark around 1902, but it was first attributed to him in an article in *Harper's Monthly* in September 1932. https://www.phrases.org.uk/meanings/genius-is-one-percent-perspiration-ninety-nine-percent-perspiration; https://www.electrochem.org/ecs-blog/tag/thomas-edison/.

5. André Gorz, *Strategy for Labor: Theories of the Labor Movement* (Detroit: Wayne State University Press, 1987), 102.

6. Anand Giriharadas, "Ro Khanna Wants Progressives to Embrace Patriotism, Aspiration, and Experimentation," *The.Ink*, February 2, 2021, https://the.ink/p/rokhanna.

7. Lee Drutman, "Trump's Election May Have Been the Shock We Needed," *New York Times*, November 25, 2019, https://www.nytimes.com/2019/11/25/opinion/trump-politics.html.

8. Fair Fight is the name of the organization that Stacey Abrams, a state senator who narrowly lost the Georgia gubernatorial race in an election widely perceived to have been marked by voter suppression, created to promote fair elections and encourage voter participation in Georgia and around the country. https://fairfight.com.

9. Compared to special interest groups, the average American citizen has little to no effect on what policies are enacted in Washington. Martin Gilens and Benjamin I. Page, "Testing Theories of American Politics: Elites, Interest Groups, and Average Citizens," *Perspectives on Politics* 12, no. 3 (2014): 564–81, https://doi.org/10.1017/S1537592714001595, cited in Katherine M. Gehl and Michael E. Porter, "Why

Competition in the Politics Industry Is Failing America: A Strategy for Reinvigorating Our Democracy" (working paper, Harvard Business School, September 2017), https://www.hbs.edu/competitiveness/Documents/why-competition-in-the -politics-industry-is-failing-america.pdf.

10. Katherine M. Gehl and Michael E. Porter, *The Politics Industry: How Political Innovation Can Break Partisan Gridlock and Save Our Democracy* (Boston: Harvard Business Review Press, 2020).

11. Lee Drutman, *Breaking the Two-Party Doom Loop: The Case for Multiparty Democracy in America* (New York: Oxford University Press, 2020).

12. Drutman, *Breaking the Two-Party Doom Loop*, 176.

13. Maine has ranked-choice voting in all federal elections and in state primaries (the Maine Supreme Court invalidated ranked-choice voting for statewide general elections). https://www.maine.gov/sos/cec/elec/upcoming/rankedchoicefaq .html. Alaska voted in 2020 to adopt ranked-choice voting for all elections. Kelsey Piper, "Alaska Voters Adopt Ranked-Choice Voting in Ballot Initiative," *Vox*, November 19, 2020, https://www.vox.com/2020/11/19/21537126/alaska-measure-2-ranked -choice-voting-results. Some twenty American cities, including New York; San Francisco; Basalt, Colorado; Eastpointe, Michigan; and Payson, Utah, have ranked-choice voting. Virginia and Utah have passed bills allowing all cities to have a ranked-choice voting option if they choose to use it. https://www.fairvote.org/where_is _ranked_choice_voting_used.

14. This was the slogan of the successful Maine campaign for ranked-choice voting, waged in the teeth of fierce opposition from both parties in the legislature and the governor.

15. Danielle S. Allen, Stephen B. Heintz, and Eric P. Liu, *Our Common Purpose: Reinventing American Democracy for the 21st Century* (Cambridge, MA: American Academy of Arts and Sciences, 2020), https://www.amacad.org/ourcommonpurpose /report.

16. Digital Undivided, "Who We Are," 2020, https://www.digitalundivided.com /about-digitalundivided.

17. League of United Latin American Citizens, "Latina Entrepreneur Academy," LULAC's Women's Empowerment (WE) Initiative, 2020, https://lulac.org /academy/.

18. Start Us Up, "America's New Business Plan," 2019, https://www.startusupnow .org/wp-content/uploads/sites/12/2019/10/Kauffman_AmericasNewBusinessPla nWhitepaper_October2019.pdf.

19. Start Us Up, "Rebuilding Better: Activating the Start Us Up Coalition in Response to Covid-19," *Covid-19 Response*, 2020, https://www.startusupnow.org/wp -content/uploads/sites/12/2020/04/Americas-New-Business-Plan-Rebuilding -Better.pdf; Start Us Up, "America's New Business Plan." This scenario is the focus of

America's New Business Plan, a bipartisan initiative that emphasizes the need for government to adopt a host of measures supportive of young businesses—those in existence five years or less—which produce most of the country's net new jobs. An entrepreneur, from this perspective, is "a person who has sold or is planning to sell a product or service, thereby entering into business and generating reportable income or expenses associated with this activity." Over the course of the pandemic (as I write this in mid-January 2021), more than two hundred incubators, accelerators, funds, and foundations have joined a coalition to "rebuild better" by implementing the recommendations in the New Business Plan.

20. Sascha Haselmayer, "Fast Tech, Slow Change," *The Commons*, January 28, 2021, https://wearecommons.us/2021/01/28/fast-tech-slow-change/.

21. "The Five Biggest Bike Share Businesses Disrupting Mobility," *Foundry4*, August 14, 2018, https://foundry4.com/the-5-biggest-bike-share-businesses-disrupting -mobility.

22. Lionel Barber, "FT Sets the Agenda with New Brand Platform," *Financial Times*, September 16, 2019, https://aboutus.ft.com/en-gb/announcements/ft-sets -the-agenda-with-new-brand-platform/; Jamie Dimon, "Business Roundtable Redefines the Purpose of a Corporation to Promote 'An Economy That Serves All Americans,'" *Business Roundtable*, August 19, 2019, https://www.businessroundtable .org/business-roundtable-redefines-the-purpose-of-a-corporation-to-promote-an -economy-that-serves-all-americans; Larry Kramer, "Beyond Neoliberalism: Rethinking Political Economy," Hewlett Foundation, April 26, 2018, https://hewlett.org /library/beyond-neoliberalism-rethinking-political-economy/; Omidyar Network, "Reimagining Capitalism," https://omidyar.com/reimagining-capitalism/; Margaret Levi, "Towards a New Moral Economy: A Thought Piece," Stanford Center for Advanced Study in the Behavioral Sciences, April 2018, https://casbs.stanford.edu /sites/g/files/sbiybj9596/f/levi-thought-piece-april-20184.pdf.

23. The best overall account of behavioral psychology is by the Nobel laureate in economics Daniel Kahneman. Daniel Kahneman, *Thinking, Fast and Slow* (New York: Farrar, Straus and Giroux, 2011).

24. One of the most often quoted passages from Aristotle is from *Politics*: "Man is by nature a political animal," who needs the city to survive. "One who is incapable of sharing or who is in need of nothing through being self-sufficient is no part of a city, and so is either a beast or a god." (*Politics* 3, 5). Fast forward several millennia to Susan Fiske, a leading social psychologist at Princeton, who describes humans as "social beings," who "are motivated to belong to groups, to develop socially shared understanding, to control their interpersonal outcomes effectively, . . . and to trust others by default." Susan T. Fiske, *Social Beings: Core Motives in Social Psychology* (Hoboken, NJ: Wiley, 2014), 35. For a popular overview of work from many different disciplines on the human need to connect with other humans, see David Brooks, *The*

Social Animal: The Hidden Sources of Love, Character, and Achievement (New York: Random House, 2011).

25. Hilary Cottam, *Radical Help: How We Can Remake the Relationships between Us and Revolutionise the Welfare State* (London: Virago, 2018).

26. Kate Raworth, *Doughnut Economics: Seven Ways to Think Like a 21st-Century Economist* (White River Junction, VT: Chelsea Green Publishing, 2017).

27. Margaret Levi, "Communities of Fate," *Edge*, 2013, https://www.edge.org /response-detail/23739.

28. See, e.g., Ai-Jen Poo, with Ariane Conrad, *The Age of Dignity: Preparing for the Elder Boom in a Changing America* (New York: New Press, 2009). For the growing "care community," see the Care 100: The Most Influential People in Care in 2020, https://www.care100list.com/.

29. Jennifer Brandel et al., "Zebras Fix What Unicorns Break," blog post, March 8, 2017, https://medium.com/zebras-unite/zebrasfix-c467e55f9d96.

30. See the full comparison chart between zebras and unicorns at https:// medium.com/zebras-unite/zebrasfix-c467e55f9d96.

31. Jennifer Brandel et al., "Pivot to People: It's Time to Build the New Economy," blog post, June 30, 2020, https://medium.com/zebras-unite/pivot-to-people-its -time-to-build-the-new-economy-75a624eaf38a.

32. https://www.springbankcollective.com/. Springbank's three founders, all graduates of Harvard Business School, are willing to say: "this amount of profit will be *enough.*" They believe that market forces can be a powerful gender equalizer, given the right investor lens. They also certainly want to earn a good living for themselves and their families, as well as for all the investors they hope to attract. Their mission, however, is more important than money alone.

33. Bernardine Evaristo, *Girl, Woman, Other: A Novel* (New York: Grove Press, 2019).

34. Pat Mitchell, *Becoming a Dangerous Woman: Embracing Risk to Change the World* (New York: Seal Press, 2019), 11.

35. Collins, *No Stopping Us Now*, 61.

36. Susan Mattern, *The Slow Moon Climbs: The Science, History, and Meaning of Menopause* (Princeton, NJ: Princeton University Press, 2019), 17.

37. Collins, *No Stopping Us Now*.

38. See Amber Christ and Tracey Gronniger, "Older Women and Poverty," Justice in Aging—Special Report, December 2018, http://www.justiceinaging.org/wp -content/uploads/2018/12/Older-Women-and-Poverty.pdf; and Monique Morrissey, "The State of American Retirement: How 401(k)s Have Failed Most American Workers," Economic Policy Institute, March 3, 2016, https://files.epi.org/2016 /state-of-american-retirement-final.pdf.

39. Alicia Menendez, *The Likeability Trap: How to Break Free and Succeed as You Are* (New York: Harper Business, 2019).

40. U.S. Bureau of Labor Statistics, "Projections of the Labor Force, 2016–26," *Career Outlook*, November 2017, https://www.bls.gov/careeroutlook/2017/article /projections-laborforce.htm.

Chapter 9: Giving and Finding Grace

1. Tyra A. Mariani, "I Chose Not to Have Children and I Couldn't Be Happier," *Time*, August 17, 2016, https://time.com/4449121/no-kids-lifestyle/.

2. Michelle Alexander, "America, This Is Your Chance," *New York Times*, June 8, 2020, https://www.nytimes.com/2020/06/08/opinion/george-floyd-protests-race .html; Michelle Alexander, *The New Jim Crow* (New York: New Press, 2012).

3. Norman Maclean, *A River Runs through It and Other Stories* (Chicago: University of Chicago Press, 2001), 31.

4. "Patagonia's North Star, Interview with Vincent Stanley," in *Resilience* (Washington, DC: New America, 2020), https://resilience.newamerica.org/patagonias -north-star/.

5. Chimamanda Ngozi Adichie, *We Should All Be Feminists* (New York: Anchor Books, 2015).

6. Loretta Ross, "I'm a Black Feminist. I Think Call-Out Culture Is Toxic," *New York Times*, August 17, 2020, https://www.nytimes.com/2019/08/17/opinion /sunday/cancel-culture-call-out.html. See additional materials on "calling in" at Ross's website, https://lorettajross.com/.

7. Ross, "I'm a Black Feminist. I Think Call-Out Culture Is Toxic."

8. Courtney E. Martin, "Preaching Faith in Democracy," *New York Times*, July 2, 2019, https://www.nytimes.com/2019/07/02/opinion/preaching-faith-in -democracy.html. See also https://citizenuniversity.us/civic-saturday/.

9. Eric Liu, *Become America: Civic Sermons on Love, Responsibility, and Democracy* (Seattle: Sasquatch Books, 2019).

10. "Civic Saturday Is a Civic Analogue to a Faith Gathering," https://citizen university.us/civic-saturday/.

Chapter 10: *Plures et Unum*

1. Fallows, *Our Towns*, 75.

2. Trabian Shorters, "Asset Framing: The Other Side of the Story," 2020, https:// www.comnetwork.org/resources/asset-framing-the-other-side-of-the-story/.

3. Trabian Shorters, "ComNet19 Keynote Address," The Communications Network, 2019. See also Ben Jealous and Trabian Shorters, eds., *Reach: 40 Black Men Speak on Living, Leading, and Succeeding* (New York: Atria Books, 2015). Also https://bmecommunity.org/.

4. Shorters, "ComNet19 Keynote Address."

5. Keith Yamashita, "This Man Turned His Life around after a Harrowing Stroke," *Oprah Magazine*, April 24, 2019.

6. Keith Yamashita, "This Tender, Unprecedented, and Universal Human Moment," blog post, April 22, 2020, https://medium.com/@keithyamashita.

7. Keith Yamashita, "Renewal: A Life Skill," blog post, April 24, 2019, https://medium.com/@keithyamashita/renewal-a-life-skill-f34611ef9f6d.

8. Lepore, *These Truths*, 623. Quoting James Baldwin as cited in Elizabeth Hinton, *From the War on Poverty to the War on Crime: The Making of Mass Incarceration in America* (Cambridge, MA: Harvard University Press, 2016).

9. For a detailed and often surprising discussion of the history of whiteness in the United States, see Painter, *The History of White People*.

10. One of the nation's top demographers, William Frey of the Brookings Institution, maps what he sees as the "diversity explosion" of the United States in the coming decades, which is very much a story of highly diverse young people and aging white Baby Boomers. Those young people will be essential "to infuse the aging American labor force with vitality and to sustain populations in many parts of the country that are facing population declines." William H. Frey, *Diversity Explosion: How New Racial Demographics Are Remaking America* (Washington, DC: Brookings Institution Press, 2014), 3.

11. William H. Frey, "The US Will Become 'Minority White' in 2045, Census Projects," blog post, March 14, 2018, https://www.brookings.edu/blog/the-avenue/2018/03/14/the-us-will-become-minority-white-in-2045-census-projects/.

12. Frey, *Diversity Explosion*, 3.

13. john a. powell and Stephen Menendian, "The Problem of Othering: Towards Inclusiveness and Belonging," *Othering and Belonging*, no. 1 (2016): 14–41, https://www.otheringandbelonging.org/wp-content/uploads/2016/07/OtheringAndBelonging_Issue1.pdf.

14. Ryan P. Williams, "Defend America—Defeat Multiculturalism," *The American Mind*, April 23, 2019, https://americanmind.org/essays/defend-america-defeat-multiculturalism/.

15. Francis Fukuyama, "Against Identity Politics: The New Tribalism and the Crisis of Democracy," *Foreign Affairs*, September/October 2018, https://www.foreignaffairs.com/articles/americas/2018-08-14/against-identity-politics-tribalism-francis-fukuyama.

16. Stacey Y. Abrams et al., "E Pluribus Unum? The Fight over Identity Politics," *Foreign Affairs*, March/April 2019, https://www.foreignaffairs.com/articles/2019-02-01/stacey-abrams-response-to-francis-fukuyama-identity-politics-article.

17. Abrams et al., "E Pluribus Unum?"

18. Abrams et al., "E Pluribus Unum?"

19. Abrams et al., "E Pluribus Unum?"

20. Langston Hughes, "Theme for English B," https://www.poetryfoundation .org/poems/47880/theme-for-english-b.

21. Pardlo, *Air Traffic*, 206.

22. Carl Schurz, "About Patriotism," *Harper's Weekly*, April 16, 1898, reprinted in *Speeches, Correspondence and Political Papers of Carl Schurz*, ed. F. Bancroft (New York: Putnam's Sons, 1913), 5:461.

23. Carl Schurz, "Remarks in the Senate," February 29, 1872, *The Congressional Globe*, 45:1287.

24. James Baldwin, *Notes of a Native Son* (Boston: Beacon Press, 2012), 34. My mentor Abram Chayes served as the State Department's top lawyer during the Kennedy Administration but later represented Nicaragua in a case against the United States for mining Nicaraguan harbors. When questioned as to how he could bring a case against his own country in the International Court of Justice, he said that he saw "nothing wrong" with "holding the United States to its own best standards and best principles." See David E. Rosenbaum, "Abram Chayes, John Kennedy Aide, Dies at 77," *New York Times*, April 18, 2000, https://www.nytimes.com/2000/04/18/us /abram-chayes-john-kennedy-aide-dies-at-77.html.

25. Nikole Hannah-Jones, "Our Democracy's Founding Ideals Were False When They Were Written: Black Americans Have Fought to Make Them True," *New York Times Magazine*, August 14, 2019, https://www.nytimes.com/interactive/2019/08 /14/magazine/black-history-american-democracy.html.

26. Hannah-Jones, "Our Democracy's Founding Ideals Were False When They Were Written."

27. Theodore Roosevelt Johnson, *When the Stars Begin to Fall: Overcoming Racism and Renewing the Promise of America* (New York: Atlantic Monthly Press, 2021), 67.

28. Anne-Marie Slaughter, "Thriving with My Birds," *Huffington Post*, May 24, 2014, https://www.huffpost.com/entry/thriving-with-my-birds_b_5020519.

29. In *The Genius of Birds* (New York: Penguin, 2016), 2, Jennifer Ackerman describes "birds that can count and do simple math, make their own tools, move to the beat of music, comprehend basic principles of physics, remember the past, and plan for the future."

30. "It is out of an egalitarian commitment that a people grows—a people that is capable of protecting us all collectively, and each of us individually, from domination." Equality and liberty together "are the summits of human empowerment; they are the twinned foundations of democracy." Danielle S. Allen, *Our Declaration: A Reading of the Declaration of Independence in Defense of Equality* (New York: Liveright, 2014), 36.

31. Allen, *Declaration*, 21.

32. Toni Morrison, "Sarah Lawrence Commencement Address," in *Mouth Full of Blood: Essays, Speeches, Meditations* (London: Vintage, 2020), 69.

33. Morrison, "Sarah Lawrence Commencement Address," 69.

34. Morrison, "Sarah Lawrence Commencement Address," 69. Italics in the original.

35. Langston Hughes wrote an entire poem titled "Dreams":

Hold fast to dreams
For if dreams die
Life is a broken-winged bird
That cannot fly.
Hold fast to dreams
For when dreams go
Life is a barren field
Frozen with snow.

Coda

1. "Read the Full Transcript of Obama's Eulogy for John Lewis," *New York Times*, July 30, 2020, https://www.nytimes.com/2020/07/30/us/obama-eulogy-john-lewis-full-transcript.html.

INDEX

THE PUBLIC SQUARE BOOK SERIES

PRINCETON UNIVERSITY PRESS